1964

Pontiac GTO

David Bonaskiewich

CarTech®

CarTech®

CarTech®, Inc.
838 Lake Street South
Forest Lake, MN 55025
Phone: 651-277-1200 or 800-551-4754
Fax: 651-277-1203
www.cartechbooks.com

Edit by Paul Johnson

ISBN 978-1-61325-320-5
Item No. CT590

Library of Congress Cataloging-in-Publication Data Available

Written, edited, and designed in the U.S.A.
Printed in China
10 9 8 7 6 5 4 3 2 1

Frontispiece:
Chrome trim that surrounds the pedals denotes a car equipped with power brakes. The lack of that trim on this GTO indicates that it is a manual-brake car. Visible at the far left next to the brake-release handle is the knob that operates the air vents located in the kick panels.

Title Page:
The Sports Coupe shared many of the same lines as the hardtop examples, but with only 7,384 Sports Coupes produced in 1964, they are highly collectible. Even when the door window is lowered, the steel frame and trim are still visible.

Contents Page:
Pontiac successfully used the tiger marketing theme through the 1966 model year. Novelty items, including the tiger tail, were yet another way that the tiger image was used in the promotion of the GTO.

DISTRIBUTION BY:

Europe
PGUK
63 Hatton Garden
London EC1N 8LE, England
Phone: 020 7061 1980 • Fax: 020 7242 3725
www.pguk.co.uk

Australia
Renniks Publications Ltd.
3/37-39 Green Street
Banksmeadow, NSW 2109, Australia
Phone: 2 9695 7055 • Fax: 2 9695 7355
www.renniks.com

Canada
Login Canada
300 Saulteaux Crescent
Winnipeg, MB, R3J-3T2, Canada
Phone: 800-665-1148 • Fax: 800-665-0103
www.LB.ca

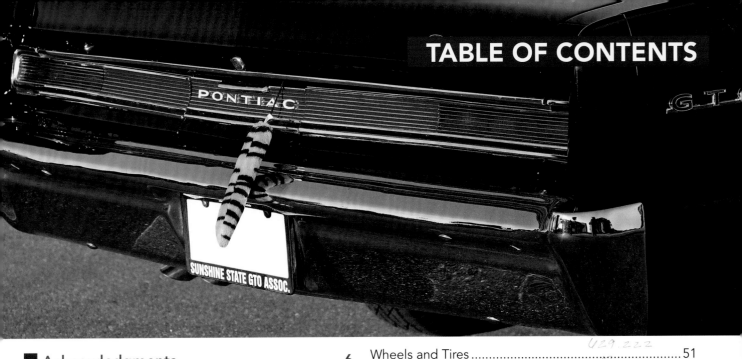

TABLE OF CONTENTS

■ **Acknowledgments**   6

■ **Introduction**   7

■ **Chapter 1: GM's New Youth Brand**   8

Base-Model Tempest...9
Bunkie Knudsen and John DeLorean 14
Inception, Design and Creation of the GTO 19
Royal Pontiac...23
Jim Wangers..26

■ **Chapter 2: A Hot Rod Tempest**   29

Tempest Standard Equipment......................30
GTO Equipment Package.............................31

■ **Chapter 3: Engine, Transmission and Rear End**   39

389 Engine...39
Tri-Power..42
Transmissions...44
Hurst Shifter...46
Rear Differential...47

■ **Chapter 4: Suspension and Brakes**   49

Suspension 49
Handling Package 51

Wheels and Tires..51
Braking System...53

■ **Chapter 5: Interior and Exterior**   57

Interior..57
Exterior 62

■ **Chapter 6: Racing**   68

Mickey Thompson 68
Drag Racing Personalities.............................71
Road Race Competitors 78

■ **Chapter 7: End of an Era**   86

Rebirth..88
Value and Collectibility.................................90
Legacy 91

■ **Appendix I: Production Figures**   94

■ **Appendix II: Interior, Exterior and Cordova/Convertible Top Colors**   94

■ **Appendix III: 1964 Pontiac LeMans Options List**   95

ACKNOWLEDGMENTS

A project such as this is a monumental task, one that surely cannot be completed by just one individual. Throughout the span of nearly a year, I've relied on many generous, knowledgeable members of the Pontiac community for fact checking, guidance, and locating prime examples of the 1964 GTO.

First and foremost, I would like to recognize all of the passionate, skilled Pontiac journalists who came before me: Paul Zazarine, Eric White, Thomas DeMauro, Christopher R. Phillip, Don Keefe, Chuck Roberts, Rocky Rotella, Gary Witzenburg, Michael Lamm, Martyn L. Schorr, Stan Rarden, Pete McCarthy, R. George Ellis, and Jeff Denison. Their expertise and devotion to the brand are unparalleled, and their combined works create the definitive library for all things Pontiac. I hope my work in this book can be added to this vast reservoir of resources available to the Pontiac enthusiast.

Christopher R. Phillip encouraged and advised me on my automotive photography and gave me the opportunity to contribute to *High Performance Pontiac* magazine, for which I am grateful. After the unfortunate demise of *High Performance Pontiac*, Chris put me in contact with Don Keefe, who was then editor of *Smoke Signals* magazine. Through Don's encouragement, I began writing feature articles, and my appetite for Pontiac history became voracious. When Don left the position at *Smoke Signals*, he created *Poncho Perfection*, a publication for which I continue to write. It was during this period that Don recommended me as a potential candidate for writing this book. Many thanks are extended to Chris and Don.

Conducting research for this book also afforded me the chance to speak with some legends in the Pontiac world. I am humbled that icons such as Arnie Beswick, Jim Wangers, Bill Collins, and Herb Adams took the time to answer my questions regarding their contributions to the 1964 Pontiac GTO. I'll be the first person to admit that I am not a proficient interviewer, sometimes struggling to get my thoughts in order, but each of these men was kind and patient during our lengthy and detailed conversations.

Behind-the-scenes individuals also assisted greatly in this project. John Viale and Andre Rayman are 1964 GTO gurus; their insight and fervor helped ensure that this book is both informative and accurate. John Kyros at GM Media Archive was pleasant and extremely helpful. My friend John S. Vick was great company when I had to travel long distances to photograph some of these wonderful GTOs. My lovely wife, Jenn, who proofread numerous drafts of each chapter, expertly extinguished any grammatical errors, and projected me in the best possible light to the folks at CarTech, Inc.

Then there are the car owners; without them this book would not have been possible, and I am very appreciative that they took the time to let me photograph their amazing cars: Terry Bagby, Cameo Ivory hardtop; Richard Capon, green modified hardtop; Steve McNutt, Marimba Red Tempest Custom; Andre Rayman, Marimba Red Sports Coupe, Saddle Bronze convertible, and Nocturne Blue convertible; Bart Dean, Starlight Black convertible; Jack Suarez, Starlight Black convertible with Hurst wheels; Brian Thomason, Gulfstream Aqua Sports Coupe; Jerry Bulger, Yorktown Blue convertible; Michael Speck, Starlight Black hardtop; David Gehr, 2006 Phantom Black GTO; Roger Williamson, 1961 Bonneville; Bobby Disher, 1962 Grand Prix.

The following people have graciously let me use their photos when time and distance prohibited me from capturing my own images: Dan Jefkins, 1963 LeMans; Dil Brandow, 1964 GTO gasser; Don Stellhorn, 1964 GTO road racer; Patty and Tony Claypool, 1959 Pontiac.

Finally, thanks to Paul Johnson at CarTech, who was with me every step of this long, rewarding journey.

Throughout my journey, compiling information and traveling to track down and photograph 1964 Pontiac GTOs, I have become somewhat of a Pontiac historian. Learning about the people, circumstances, and obstacles regarding the development of this model only served to enhance my appreciation for this legendary car.

Upon telling members of the Pontiac community that I was writing a book on the 1964 GTO, a recurring question was, "How are you going to differentiate it from all the other books on the topic?" A fair question and one that I have pondered for quite some time. First, this book has to cover all the basic facts about the car that may have been in previous publications; it would be incomplete otherwise. Second, this book is meant to serve as a guide to both the seasoned Pontiac aficionado and those new to the hobby.

In addition, I believe that the fresh photography and my personal interpretation of interviews with Pontiac legends offer some different and useful perspectives to readers. I've also included a great deal of general Pontiac history, showing the tremendous progress that the brand made from the mid-1950s to the genesis of the 1964 GTO. I am particularly proud of the piece regarding the Gray Ghost Trans-Am series race car. It is a very cool part of the GTO's legacy and I think you will thoroughly enjoy it.

It is my goal that this book becomes an invaluable resource to anyone seeking knowledge on the 1964 GTO. I have learned a lot over the past year researching this book and, in addition to facts and figures, have tried to include everything that I personally found curious or interesting. I've done my very best to separate fact from conjecture and hearsay. There are some topics about the 1964 model that are not known definitively, and I've tried to make that clear within the text, where applicable.

Respected Pontiac journalist Don Keefe sums up the 1964 GTO quite nicely: "The Pontiac GTO is considered by many to be the first muscle car, and I completely agree with that assessment. While there were previous cars that offered powerful engines in lighter body styles, such as the Buick Century of the 1930s, the Chrysler 300 of the 1950s, and even the V-8 Rambler, the GTO was different. There were even factory-built race cars that came along in the early 1960s that were faster: the Max Wedge Mopar lightweights and Pontiac's own Super Duty cars come to mind.

"To my mind, though, the 1964 Pontiac GTO earns its 'original muscle car' status because it was the first time that a high-performance engine from a full-size car line was installed in an intermediate chassis *and* was marketed specifically to younger buyers with an advertising and promotional campaign that emphasized street performance as opposed to out-and-out racing. The engines in the GTO were powerful but were, in actuality, fairly mild engines, with hydraulic cams and inexpensive cast bottom-end pieces. The lack of exotic componentry meant that these cars could remain affordable and appeal to a wide base of buyers.

"History certainly proved that John DeLorean, Bill Collins, and Russ Gee knew what they were doing!"

CHAPTER 1

GM'S NEW YOUTH BRAND

Pontiacs, such as this striking 1961 Bonneville, were built on the success of the highly acclaimed 1959 Wide Track models. The combination of style, luxury, and performance became a hallmark for Pontiac Motor Division throughout the 1960s, 1970s, and beyond.

The full-size Pontiacs of the late 1950s and early 1960s played an indirect but important role in the GTO's development. The Catalina, Ventura, Bonneville, and later, the Grand Prix, were available with high-performance engine, transmission, and rear-end combinations. These iconic machines were instrumental in crafting Pontiac's performance image at a crucial time when the fate of the brand was uncertain.

Famed Pontiac ad man Jim Wangers recalls, "Pontiac had a great product but didn't realize how good it was. They had a nice, simple overhead-valve V-8 with a lot of torque. The 316-ci engine was okay, but it was easy for people to write off. With the 347 debuting in 1957, the cars took a giant step forward, and people started noticing." Sales began to rise, and Pontiac increased its involvement in various types of motor-

sports. In fact, many of these large B-Body cars could be found blasting down quarter-mile dragstrips or competing in stock-car races, dominating the competition with Pontiac power.

In 1957, Cotton Owens recorded Pontiac's first win in stock-car racing on the beach course at Daytona. A few years later, legendary NASCAR driver Fireball Roberts won both races at Daytona International Speedway in 1962, driving his famous black and gold Pontiac, tuned by notable mechanic Smokey Yunick. It was the beginning of a very exciting and prosperous era for Pontiac Motor Division.

The engine that eventually became synonymous with the 1964 GTO, the 389-ci Tri-Power, was first introduced in 1959 and proved to be popular with new-car buyers seeking to inject some excitement into

Full-size Pontiacs from the early 1960s were high performing and attractive. Models such as the 1962 Grand Prix could be viewed as inspiration for the 1964 Tempest, LeMans, and GTO. Jet black with gold accents, this Grand Prix is a Fireball Roberts tribute car and packs the additional punch of a 421 Super Duty engine and 4-speed transmission.

their driving experience. The all-new 1959 Pontiacs were completely restyled and well received by automotive critics and the general public alike. The engine remained available through the 1966 model year, when it was replaced with the 400-ci engine in 1967, and the Tri-Power induction system was discontinued.

Many of the 1964 GTO's styling cues arose from the 1962 full-size Pontiacs, particularly the Grand Prix. Clean, sharp body lines, four horizontal headlights, and the restrained use of exterior chrome trim contributed to an overall masculine profile, themes that were all visible in the GTO's first year of production.

For 1964, full-size Pontiacs and smaller midsize units, such as the GTO, were given similar attention in terms of available performance combinations. Numerous high-output engine options could be ordered in the Grand Prix, Catalina, and Bonneville, culminating with the 421 H.O. This mill displayed a hefty 370 hp and 460 ft-lbs of torque, and the GTO could be had with the 389 Tri-Power, which boasted 348 hp and 428 ft-lbs of axle-twisting torque. Although horsepower numbers crept up a bit in 1965, the focus of the large B-Body

cars gravitated toward luxury rather than performance, and thanks to an innovative and aggressive marketing campaign, the GTO rapidly became known as Pontiac's high-performance model.

BASE-MODEL TEMPEST

It is widely known that the GTO used the midsize 1964 Pontiac Tempest as a foundation. However, to fully appreciate its design, performance, and lasting influence, we must trace its true origin to the 1961 Tempest, a compact and intriguing entry-level automobile.

Conceptualized by John DeLorean, and very innovative for the time, this low-priced Pontiac featured a front engine and rear-mounted transaxle, eliminating the transmission "hump" in the floorpan and increasing passenger legroom. In addition, this format resulted in near-perfect weight distribution. Power was transmitted via a flexible driveshaft housed within a separate tunnel called a torque tube, differentiating it from the otherwise similar Oldsmobile F-85 and Buick Special, each of which displayed a conventional front-mounted engine

The 1964 Tempest was the perfect platform for Pontiac to build its new supercar, the GTO, setting the stage for the American muscle car phenomenon. This Marimba Red 1964 Tempest Custom features the 215-ci inline 6-cylinder engine.

At first glance, the 195-ci 4-cylinder could easily be mistaken for a V-8 engine, and in fact, it was exactly half of one. This represented yet another example of Pontiac's resourcefulness in providing a quality product while keeping production costs to a minimum.

OPPOSITE: Pontiac's highly innovative engineers focused on differentiating the early Tempests from GM's other compact offerings in terms of both mechanics and aesthetics. Today, the 1961 and 1962 Pontiac Tempests are quite rare and thereby coveted by many automotive collectors. This 1962 Tempest LeMans convertible would be a valued addition to any Pontiac enthusiast's garage.

In addition to upgraded interior appointments, the Tempest LeMans featured distinctive badging and could be ordered with full wheel covers. The large 15-inch wheels were unique within GM's compact lineup; other divisions used the more common 14-inch size.

The Pontiac Tempest and LeMans were completely restyled for 1963. The optional 326-ci engine replaced the 215-ci Buick V-8 that could be ordered in the 1961 and 1962 models. The 326-ci shared the same stroke as the larger 389-ci, with a smaller bore of 3.78 inches, and after 1963, 3.72 inches. (Photo Courtesy Dan Jefkins)

and transmission. Foregoing a traditional perimeter frame, these three models were built with unibody construction, primarily for greater cost and weight savings.

Power for the early Tempests came from a 195-ci inline 4-cylinder. Known as the "Trophy 4," the engine was derived from the passenger-side cylinder bank of the popular 389 V-8, allowing Pontiac to minimize manufacturing expenses. Three versions were available: a low-compression 1-barrel carburetor rated at 110 hp, a high-compression 1-barrel at 140 hp, and a high-compression 4-barrel pumping out 155 hp.

An interesting option for the 1961 and 1962 Tempest was the availability of the 215-ci Buick aluminum V-8. Installed in approximately 1 percent of Tempests, this small engine produced 155 hp and 220 ft-lbs of torque. With its many unique characteristics, the 1961

Pontiac Tempest rightfully earned the *Motor Trend* Car of the Year award.

In late 1961, the Tempest LeMans model was introduced as an alternative to the sparsely equipped Tempest. Essentially a trim package, it consisted of front bucket seats in place of the more conventional bench seat found in the Tempest and could be ordered for the two-door coupe and convertible models. By 1962, the Tempest was available in a full array of configurations: convertible, two-door coupe, four-door sedan, and four-door station wagon.

The 1963 models still rode on the same 112-inch wheelbase as the 1961 and 1962 units but wore completely new sheet metal and gained about 5 inches in overall length. Advertised as a "Senior Compact," the

The 1964 Pontiac Tempest was available in various trim levels: a base model, the Tempest Custom, and the Tempest LeMans. This Tempest Custom features a vinyl top and full wheel covers.

A close relative to the Chevrolet 230 inline 6-cylinder engine, the 215-ci was unique to Pontiac Motor Division. A reliable powerplant, it was produced in 1964 and 1965, until it was replaced with the innovative overhead-cam engine in 1966.

1963 Tempest could now be optioned with a powerful 326-ci V-8 engine, producing 260 hp and 352 ft-lbs of torque, and a stronger transaxle was developed to accommodate its power. The 326-ci proved to be a popular choice in 1963, with more than half of all LeMans units using this engine. Although the actual displacement was 336 ci, it was advertised as 326 to remain below the 330-ci limit for GM compact cars.

The 1963 Tempest and LeMans clearly conveyed a transition from the smaller, economy-based 1961–1962 models to the larger 1964 models and foreshadowed what became one of the most significant cars in the history of Pontiac Motor Division.

The 1964 model year brought about major changes for the Tempest and LeMans. No longer a compact, the unibody construction was replaced with a full-perimeter frame and the wheelbase increased to 115 inches, with an overall length of 203 inches. A completely redesigned exterior gave the Tempest and LeMans a more chiseled and muscular aesthetic. Now designated as the A-Body, it shared the same chassis as the Buick Skylark, Oldsmobile Cutlass, and Chevrolet Chevelle and featured a more conventional front-mounted engine and transmission.

A 215-ci inline 6-cylinder producing 140 hp replaced the 195-ci 4-cylinder as the base engine. Although the popular 326-ci V-8 remained in the lineup, its bore was reduced to 3.71875 inches, which resulted in a true displacement of 326 ci.

In 1964, Pontiac Motor Division offered three separate models for its A-Body lineup: 20-Series Tempest, 21-Series Tempest Custom, and 22-Series Tempest LeMans. The LeMans package included a Deluxe steering wheel, partially carpeted door panels, additional cabin lighting, and bucket seats. Sales figures were very strong, with 202,676 combined units produced, including the Tempest, Tempest Custom, and Tempest LeMans, excluding the GTO.

BUNKIE KNUDSEN AND JOHN DELOREAN

In the mid-1950s, Pontiac was building dependable, yet underwhelming vehicles, resulting in a sixth-place market position. This brought about rumors that Pontiac

The owner of this 1964 Tempest custom still possesses the original owner's manual with a note reading, "Chassis lubricated every 12,000 miles if Pontiac grease is used. Other grease, every 6,000 miles." Also shown is the IDENT-O-PLATE, a small metal plate containing pertinent information specific to the car used at the dealer for warranty claims.

Bunkie Knudsen and his team were making a deliberate effort to move away from large, Indian-themed ornamentation such as this. In addition, one of Knudsen's first decisions at Pontiac was to remove the Silver Streak trim that adorned countless Pontiacs from the 1940s and 1950s.

could be absorbed by the more successful Oldsmobile brand. However, with a new management team and a fresh, exciting perspective, Pontiac soon produced some of America's most legendary and sought-after automobiles.

Semon "Bunkie" Knudsen was born October 2, 1912, in Buffalo, New York. The son of former GM president William S. Knudsen, Bunkie had an interest in automobiles from an early age, even assembling his first car from components his father had given him as a test of his abilities. Knudsen accepted and completed this and many other challenges, eventually graduating from the Massachusetts Institute of Technology in 1936. After graduation, he found employment with local machine

The 1959 models were the first of the "Wide-Track" Pontiacs. In addition to performance benefits, the wider width offered Pontiac a unique focus for its new marketing strategy. Renowned artists Art Fitzpatrick and Van Kaufman created many of Pontiac's advertisements from the Wide-Track era, tastefully exaggerating the low, wide appearance. (Photo Courtesy Don Keefe)

Along with a dramatic new body, cabins of the 1959 Pontiacs were also restyled. The Bonneville represented the top trim level for Pontiac, displaying a timeless elegance that further enhanced the brand's new direction. (Photo Courtesy Don Keefe)

Semon "Bunkie" Knudsen proudly poses with two 1961 Pontiacs. Knudsen, along with Pete Estes and John DeLorean, transformed Pontiac into a performance brand and set the stage for the arrival of the 1964 GTO. (Photo Courtesy GM Media Archive)

JOHN DELOREAN

The storied life of John Zachary DeLorean began January 6, 1925, in the Motor City: Detroit, Michigan. DeLorean's father, Zachary, was a Romanian immigrant who worked for Ford Motor Company, and his mother, Kathryn, worked for General Electric. Although financially stable, at least by Depression-era standards, the DeLorean household was a turbulent one, and the couple eventually divorced in 1942.

Despite considerable challenges at home, John was an exceptional student, earning a scholarship to the Lawrence Institute of Technology. However, because of World War II, his education was put on hold, and in 1943 he was drafted into the military, serving three years in the U.S. Army. Upon returning home, he resumed his collegiate pursuits and graduated in 1948 with a degree in industrial engineering. At the behest of John's uncle, Earl Pribak, DeLorean entered the Chrysler Institute of Engineering and graduated in 1952 with a degree in automotive engineering. He was briefly employed by Chrysler before accepting a position at Packard Motor Company, where he worked alongside Forest McFarland, refining his engineering and design skills.

By 1956, John DeLorean was already a valuable commodity and accepted a position at Pontiac as an assistant to general manager Bunkie Knudsen and chief engineer Pete Estes. DeLorean said, "I was offered jobs in five different divisions of General Motors and eventually decided on Pontiac. The main reason for my decision was the general manager of the division, Semon E. 'Bunkie' Knudsen."

DeLorean rose quickly through the ranks, advancing to chief engineer at Pontiac in 1961. Due in part to the major success of the 1964 GTO, he was then appointed general manager of Pontiac Motor Division in 1965 at age 40, the youngest person to hold such a title. Some of DeLorean's other Pontiac achievements

A gifted man with a flair for style, John DeLorean was perhaps the most instrumental figure in the development of the 1964 Pontiac GTO. His passion for the brand, combined with his engineering experience and creativity, led him to become one of the most influential men in the history of General Motors. (Photo Courtesy GM Media Archive)

included the 1967 Firebird and the beautifully redesigned 1969 Grand Prix. The restyled Grand Prix was a major success, selling 112,486 units compared to the 1968 model, which sold a dismal 37,711 copies. DeLorean was later moved to the Chevrolet division in 1969, where he had success with the Monte Carlo and Camaro. However, it wasn't long before DeLorean's renegade mentality clashed with members of GM's upper management, and he left the company in 1973. After his career at General Motors, he is remembered primarily for his namesake car, the DeLorean DMC-12.

shops before landing at General Motors in 1939 as a tool engineer.

In 1956, Knudsen became the youngest general manager in GM history when he was promoted to head of Pontiac at age 43. With Pontiac on the verge of extinction, Knudsen was assigned the task of improving sales. He recruited the talents of Pete Estes from the Oldsmobile division as chief engineer and John DeLorean, from Packard, as director of advanced design. It's not an overstatement that the creative thinking, hard work, and enthusiasm of Knudsen, Estes, and DeLorean saved Pontiac from a much earlier demise than the brand ultimately experienced in 2010.

A striking automobile from all angles, the 1959 Pontiac helped the brand break away from its previous workaday image. Robust sales figures for the 1959 models proved that Bunkie Knudsen and his team were leading Pontiac Motor Division into an exciting new era. (Photo Courtesy Tony Claypool)

At the Automobile Manufacturers Association meeting in June 1957, Harlow Curtice, then-president of General Motors, considered a voluntary ban on factory racing involvement. This was due in part to the tragedy at the 1955 24 Hours of Le Mans race, where a car piloted by Pierre Levegh careened into the stands, killing more than 80 people and injuring dozens more. Curtice reasoned that this self-imposed measure would prevent the U.S. government from issuing a stricter mandatory ban. Some automakers adhered closely to the new racing policy, but Knudsen, needing every advantage if he were to resuscitate Pontiac, ultimately chose to go racing.

With the trio of Knudsen, Estes, and DeLorean now firmly established, Pontiac focused its attention on younger car buyers who were looking for something new and exciting. Knudsen once said, "You can sell a young man's car to an old man, but you can't sell an old man's car to a young man." Knudsen and his youthful colleagues' first major accomplishments were the 1959 Wide-Track Pontiacs, which were a radical departure from the 1957 and 1958 models. This complete rede-

sign included all-new sheet metal, and it was edgier and more streamlined than ever before. It also introduced the now-iconic split grill design featured on every Pontiac except the 1960 models. The 1959 "Wide-Tracks" got their name because the wheels were brought outward about 5 inches, a design sparked by Charles M. Jordan. The change resulted in a more aggressive appearance and an automobile that handled much better than its predecessors.

In an interview for *High Performance Pontiac* magazine with respected Pontiac journalist, Thomas A. DeMauro, Knudsen remembers, "The 1959 model was new from the ground up and had an entirely different look. It was wider, longer, and sleeker. The chassis was completely new, used an updated rear suspension system, and was much better suited to racing than the previous model." The 1959s were well received, earning the *Motor Trend* Car of the Year award and fueling sales growth of more than 56 percent.

Despite the voluntary 1957 AMA racing ban, Knudsen was able to maintain Pontiac's strong presence at NASCAR and drag race venues across the country. Racing legends Smokey Yunick, Fireball Roberts, Mickey Thompson, and many others took Pontiacs to the winner's circle and helped shed the old Pontiac image. With a performance reputation now steadily growing, new-car sales continued to increase, propelling Pontiac to third place in overall sales in 1962, behind only Chevrolet and Ford.

In recognition of his proven success at Pontiac, Bunkie Knudsen was promoted to general manager of Chevrolet in 1961, while Pete Estes assumed that role for Pontiac, and John DeLorean moved to chief engineer at 36 years old, the youngest person to hold that position. Although Knudsen did a tremendous job of crafting Pontiac into a well-respected performance brand, his direct involvement with the GTO extended only to the hiring of DeLorean, Estes, and a few other key people.

INCEPTION, DESIGN AND CREATION OF THE GTO

In addition to the 1957 Automobile Manufacturer Association's ban on racing, General Motors instituted its own prohibition on motorsports in 1963. By that time, Pontiac was highly involved in both NASCAR and drag race competition; the 1963 ban necessitated a new strategy if Pontiac were to remain a performance-oriented brand. Pete Estes and John DeLorean devised a new approach: street performance.

The handsome, redesigned exterior of the 1964 Tempests, combined with Pontiac's decision to return to the front-mounted engine and transmission layout, proved to be wise, selling 235,126 (GTOs included) units in 1964, compared with 131,490 in 1963. The 326-ci V-8 was a solid performer, with the 2-barrel engine producing 250 hp and the 4-barrel 326 H.O. boasting 280 hp.

With attention now focused on automobiles built for youthful, thrill-seeking car buyers, it didn't take long for Pontiac's young management team to once again push the envelope for what could be accomplished within the confines of the strict upper management rules and regulations of General Motors.

Pontiac had officially withdrawn from racing in 1963, but John DeLorean and his team wanted to continue building upon the performance image that the brand cultivated under Bunkie Knudsen. The 1964 GTO filled a crucial role within the division and brought Pontiac performance to the streets.

The Pontiac GTO almost certainly would not have existed without the contributions of both Bill Collins and Russell Gee; the ideas and technical expertise of Bill (a chassis engineer) and Russell (an engine specialist) were integral in the development of the car.

Bill Collins

Bill Collins' affinity for automobiles began at a very early age. His father was a mechanic at a Ford dealership and Bill remembers, "When I was a little kid, he would take me down there on Saturdays. I think that's where my interest in cars began." Bill later attained his mechanical engineering degree from Lehigh University in Bethlehem, Pennsylvania, and began his career at Pontiac Motor Division soon thereafter. He tested acceleration and fuel economy on the "new for 1955" V-8 engines before serving two years in the U.S. Army.

Upon returning to General Motors in 1958, Bill Collins recalls, "The difference between Pontiac in 1954 and 1958 was monumental. George Delaney was in charge of Pontiac in 1954 and he was very old-school and kind of set in his ways, while Pete Estes was much more current and performance

Bill Collins was instrumental in developing the 1963 Pontiac Tempest Super Duty cars, wherein driveline components were strengthened to withstand racing conditions. This menacing example pays homage to those legendary machines. (Photo Courtesy Dan Jefkins)

This 1963 Ferrari 250 GTO is similar to the cars that many automotive and racing experts believed would dominate the 1963 Challenge Cup race in Daytona Beach, Florida. However, thanks in part to Bill Collins, the number-50 Pontiac Tempest, driven by Paul Goldsmith, proved to be the dominant car at the track on that historic day.

oriented." Collins was in charge of designing and testing the transaxles for the 1961 Tempest, later developing upgrades for the units that were required to handle the power of the stout 421 Super Duty engines that were installed in 14 1963 Tempests.

Most of these Tempests were drag race cars, but one was modified for circle track usage. Collins recalls, "I was very involved with the 1963 Super Duty Tempests and the famous race at Daytona that included two Ferrari GTOs. The GM racing ban in 1963 eventually killed that series for us."

That "famous race" was the Daytona 250-mile Challenge Cup, and the 1963 Tempest driven by Paul Goldsmith not only lapped the Ferrari driven by David Piper, but finished first, a full 5 miles ahead of second-place finisher, A. J. Foyt. Famed NASCAR driver Fireball Roberts finished fourth, behind the wheel of a Ferrari GTO. The Goldsmith-piloted Tempest had a top speed of 163 mph and led 74 of the 100 laps.

Bill Collins was promoted to assistant chief engineer at Pontiac in 1967 and stayed with the company until 1974. In a recent phone interview, he said, "I actually suggested that Pontiac drop the GTO after the 1974 model. They went from the LeMans body style in 1973 to the Nova X-Body in 1974 as a way to further reduce costs. Sales departments were not performance oriented and just wanted to sell cars."

Collins then went to work for John DeLorean, co-designing the iconic DMC-12 model. He later founded his own company, Vixen Motorhome, in 1981. Vixens are known as the "driver's RV" and are well respected for their innovative design, including a low center of gravity, fuel-efficient engine, and the ability to be housed in a conventional garage.

Russell Gee

As an engine specialist, Russell Gee was another key component in the genesis of the 1964 GTO. In

With the external dimensions of the 389-ci engine the same as the 326-ci, installing the larger engine was a simple task for Pontiac engineers. Later, other GM brands followed the same formula of fitting large-displacement engines in midsize chassis. However, engines such as Chevrolet's 396-ci big-block were physically much larger than the brand's 283-ci and 327-ci small-blocks and required more effort for the installation.

1956, he was testing Pontiac's V-8 engine for durability when Bunkie Knudsen and Pete Estes approached him. Their goal was to enter Pontiac in stock car racing, and they appointed Gee head of the program. Working with other engineers, Gee was able to vastly improve the car's performance and increase power output from the 347 engine. These efforts were rewarded in the form of several NASCAR victories from 1957 to 1962.

With Gee now fluent in performance Pontiacs, he regularly accompanied John DeLorean and Bill Collins at the Pontiac (GM) testing facility. Staring at the 326 engine in a 1964 Tempest, Bill Collins said, "You know, John, it would take us about a half hour to stick a 389

in this thing." With the external dimensions of the 326 and 389 being exactly the same, it was a simple task for the crew, and the new engine was installed and ready for next week's session.

Collins says, "Russell Gee was in charge of the engine and machine shops, and he and his guys did the installation. Pontiac was very small in those days and all of us had 'overall car experience,' not just one area of expertise, which was a big advantage."

Gee stayed with Pontiac until 1979, when he accepted a position at Chevrolet as head of the racing and performance programs.

John DeLorean held regular brainstorming sessions with his top men at the GM Proving Grounds, a testing and tuning facility where he and engineers including Russell Gee and Bill Collins could try new ideas and concepts. Collins recalls, "When I made the suggestion of installing the 389 engine in the Tempest, my idea was to adapt the car for NASCAR competition, but John DeLorean and Jim Wangers took it in a completely different direction." Although a 389 Tempest never materialized for NASCAR, Collins' brilliant idea of installing a large engine in a midsize chassis soon had all other American manufacturers trying to keep pace with the Pontiac GTO.

Fun, spirited driving is part of what made the 1964 GTO so popular. John DeLorean knew that he had a winner when he had difficulty getting his own 1964 model back from friends after loaning it to them.

In his autobiography, DeLorean wrote, "I have always enjoyed driving high-powered, exciting cars. To put a little excitement in my drive back and forth to work, I had taken a Tempest, Pontiac's compact car, and dumped a triple 2-barrel 389 in it, and added heavy-duty shocks, roll bars, and a Hurst shifter. The car was so much fun to drive that when I loaned it to friends, I could never get it back."

Pete Estes loved the idea of a high-performing, midsize Pontiac and approved the idea without consulting upper management, fearing they would reject the concept. To get the 1964 GTO into production, it was marketed as a $295.90 option on the LeMans, rather than a separate model; unlike a completely new model, an option on an existing unit did not require approval from the conservative top-level management.

For their $295.90, adrenaline-seeking buyers received a 325-hp 389 engine topped with a single Carter AFB 4-barrel carburetor, dual exhaust, and 3.23 rear-end gears. A Hurst unit handled shifting on both the 3- and 4-speed manual transmissions. Tri-Power induction was optional and featured three 2-barrel carburetors. The Tri-Power was rated at 348 hp and boasted the added benefit of being visually impressive.

Even though John DeLorean and his team were enthusiastic about the GTO, others in the division weren't as keen. DeLorean once said, "Frank Bridge, the sales manager, bet me a dinner that we wouldn't sell 5,000 cars, but we ended up selling 31,000 that year." Official sales figures are even higher: 32,450 Pontiac GTOs sold in 1964.

ROYAL PONTIAC

Royal Pontiac played a key role in the development of the GTO. The man behind Royal Pontiac was Asa Wilson Jr., nicknamed "Ace." He was born into a wealthy family that made its money with a dairy farm. Sensing his son's lack of interest in the family business, Asa Wilson Sr. bought Ace a Pontiac dealership in Royal Oak, Michigan.

The relationship between Pontiac Motor Division and the Royal Pontiac dealership can be traced to September 1959, when Jim Wangers approached Asa Wilson Jr. with the idea that his dealership would be a facility where Pontiac could market, sell, and install performance parts. Ace Wilson was more than receptive to the notion, and Wangers stated, "He was so enthusiastic about it, he went ballistic and would not let me out of his office until he signed a contract." Located just 15 miles outside of Detroit, it was the perfect place to conduct a race-inspired business and has since become synonymous with Pontiac Performance.

A red 1959 Catalina driven by Bill Sidwell became the first Royal Pontiac race car and boasted a 389-ci engine with 345 hp and 425 ft-lbs of torque. The 389 was treated to an array of performance upgrades and ran quite well, but the column-shifted 3-speed manual transmission proved to be cumbersome and the crew eventually installed a 4.88:1 rear end, enabling Sidwell to launch the car in second gear and requiring only one shift in the quarter-mile.

After an accident on the street involving Sidwell and the 1959 Catalina race car, Jim Wangers assumed driving duties for the Royal racing team. He piloted a 1960 Catalina (with a floor-mounted, 4-speed manual transmission) to victory in the Top Stock Eliminator class at the U.S. Nationals in 1960. He is credited with the idea of using the name "Bobcat," formed by rearranging the letters from the Catalina and Bonneville models. A white 1961 Catalina served as the first official Royal race car to use that moniker and came equipped with the 348-hp 389 engine with Tri-Power induction. Royal Pontiac quickly became the unofficial test dealership for Pontiac Motor Division, gaining a solid reputation for extracting the most power out of the 389, and later, the 421 engines.

Milt Schornack was a talented young mechanic from Detroit who began working at Royal Pontiac in October 1963 and became an integral contributor to the Royal Bobcat team. In Keith J. MacDonald's book, *Milt Schornack and the Royal Bobcat GTOs*, Schornack

Jim Wangers first approached Bill Packer Jr. of Packer Pontiac with his idea for a performance-based dealership. A deal wasn't reached with Packer but instead with Wangers' second choice, Royal Pontiac. Even today, enthusiasts continue to adorn their beloved, classic machines with Royal Pontiac livery, saluting the most famous Pontiac dealership of them all.

A 1963 Pontiac Catalina speeds down the boulevard. Wearing period-correct lettering and distinctive eight-lug wheels, it's a throwback to the time when Pontiac dominated both street and track.

recalls, "The first project they put me on at Royal was the Royal Bobcat Tempest, which was actually a station wagon with a 421 Super Duty engine." Milt performed a complete teardown and rebuild of the engine and was soon working with senior Royal Bobcat mechanics Bud Conrad and Chuck Brumfield.

Royal Bobcat performance tunes became popular with non-professional street racers who wanted to dominate the boulevards of the Motor City and its surrounding areas; eventually, a Bobcat "kit" could be mail-ordered and a competent car owner could have it installed over the course of a weekend. Schornack states, "I want everyone to know that I didn't introduce the Bobcat package. That claim belongs to Frank Rediker, Wynn Brown, Dick Jesse, and another salesman at Royal Pontiac, John Martin."

The Royal Bobcat kit included various fine-tuning components such as a distributor re-curve kit that came with new points, a condenser, and lighter weights and springs. The buyer also received thinner cylinder head gaskets to raise the compression ratio, locking rocker arm nuts, and new valvecover gaskets. New carburetor jets and an intake manifold gasket to block the heat riser for a cooler air/fuel mixture completed the package.

Although the mail-order kit was a huge success, "in-house" packages, which were more thorough and custom tailored to each vehicle, remained popular with serious performance enthusiasts. Schornack stated, "Those Pontiac engines just loved compression, so when you combined the shaved heads with the thinner head gaskets, you'd decrease head-to-block clearance by about .035 inch. This would increase the compression ratio to a true 11:1." At its peak in 1966, Royal Pontiac sold approximately 1,000 Bobcat conversions.

The Royal Bobcat program enjoyed continued success throughout the 1960s, including a pair of race-ready 1966 GTOs called the GeeTO Tigers, which were accompanied at most events by a mascot clad in a tiger suit. Ever-increasingly radical ideas, such as installing the new 428-ci engine into the redesigned 1968 GTO, became the stuff of legend.

By the late 1960s, the daily responsibilities of running an automotive dealership began to take their toll on Asa Wilson Jr. He became frustrated by internal dealership politics and eventually sold Royal Pontiac in 1970 to John DeLorean's brother, George.

Royal Pontiac quickly became known as the "go-to" dealership for Pontiac performance upgrades. In addition to internal modifications, this engine was treated to an aftermarket intake and two 4-barrel carburetors, a common sight in the 1960s.

JIM WANGERS

While John DeLorean, Russell Gee, and Bill Collins are credited with the creation of the GTO, much of the early success of the car can be attributed to famed marketing guru, Jim Wangers, whose energetic and relentless advertising campaigns convincingly portrayed the Pontiac GTO as the epitome of a high-performance street machine. Without Wangers' relentless promotion in dealerships, at racetracks, in print ads, and even on television and radio, the Pontiac GTO would never have become the legend that it is today.

Wangers was born in Chicago, Illinois, and displayed an enthusiasm for cars at a very young age. Near the climax of World War II, Wangers voluntarily enlisted in the U.S. Navy, where he was a radio operator on the USS *Bunker Hill*. His time in the service was relatively uneventful, as the ship was eventually used to transport American troops back to the United States after the war.

Back home in Chicago, Wangers attended the Illinois Institute of Technology with the hope of becoming an automotive engineer. Struggling, he realized that engineering wasn't his forte, and he soon enrolled in a liberal arts school and graduated in 1949 with a bachelor's degree in English. He then accepted a position at *Esquire* magazine, promoting its *Coronet* publication and working alongside a young Hugh Hefner. Wangers turned down an offer to work for Hefner on his new venture, *Playboy* magazine, citing his desire to work in the automotive field.

Bill Weintraub was one of the founders of *Esquire*, and later started his own ad agency, W. H. Weintraub & Company. At Weintraub, Wangers landed his dream job of working in the automotive industry for Kaiser Motors. One of his first assignments was to market the Kaiser supercharged, flathead 6-cylinder engine as a superior alternative to the competition's V-8s.

Realizing that a supercharged engine performs very well at higher altitudes, Wangers pioneered the concept of using the Kaiser to attempt to break the Pikes Peak hill climb record. Although it was a brilliant idea, management deemed it too costly. Financially strapped Kaiser eventually became fragmented and produced its final passenger car in 1955, lacking the resources to keep pace with the larger manufacturers.

Upon Kaiser's demise, Wangers soon found a job at Campbell-Ewald, Chevrolet's advertising agency. Witnessing firsthand the dominance of the 1955 Chevys at Daytona, Wangers was instrumental in promoting the new Chevrolet performance image. To help push the 1956 models, he pitched his unused Pikes Peak hill climb idea, and the new Chevrolets conquered the mountain, shattering the old record and solidifying Chevrolet as a performance brand.

In 1958, after two years of working for Chrysler, Wangers accepted a position with Pontiac's advertising agency, MacManus, John & Adams. With Bunkie Knudsen at the helm, and the new 1959 models set to debut, it was a very exciting time to be involved with the Pontiac brand.

Sensing a great opportunity, Wangers pressed Knudsen and his colleagues to educate Pontiac dealers nationwide about the potential profit and publicity that racing and performance could provide. Knudsen agreed and prompted Wangers to pursue a relationship with a Pontiac dealer that could specialize in the sale and

An icon in the automotive marketing world, Jim Wangers pioneered many aggressive and highly successful advertising campaigns for Pontiac. Currently residing in Oceanside, California, Wangers remains an enthusiastic presence in the Pontiac community. (Photo Courtesy Dave Anderson)

installation of high-performance parts and equipment. Royal Pontiac in Royal Oak, Michigan, became the dealer of choice and was vital to the success of Pontiac throughout the 1960s.

When the 1964 Pontiac GTO was conceived, Wangers was already an experienced marketing guru and proved to be invaluable to the branding of the model. With an initial run of just 5,000 units, Wangers and the rest of the Pontiac team decided not to overhype the GTO, still fearful that upper management could cancel the project at any time. We know now that the 1964 GTO went on to great acclaim, much of that due to the creative and tireless efforts of Jim Wangers.

In the December 1963 issue of *Hot Rod* magazine, editor Ray Brock test drove a base engine 1964 convertible with a 2-speed automatic transmission and 3.23:1 rear-end gearing. Although he praised certain aspects of the new Pontiac, Brock was seemingly underwhelmed by the GTO's performance, stating that the 2-speed automatic "certainly put a damper on an obviously powerful engine."

Although the *Hot Rod* article wasn't overly critical, it lacked the high praise that Wangers was striving to cultivate and prompted him to approach John DeLorean, requesting that two cars be provided specifically for the automotive press. DeLorean agreed and two coupes were built and given the Royal Bobcat treatment, ensuring that journalists would be test-driving a "proper" GTO and more likely to speak favorably of it.

The now-famous issue of *Car and Driver* magazine from March 1964 depicted a Pontiac GTO in hot pursuit of the Ferrari 250 GTO, with a line that read: "Tempest GTO: 0 to 100 in 11.8 seconds." Wangers envisioned a head-to-head duel between the Pontiac and Ferrari GTOs, whereby a winner would be crowned following a series of performance tests in Daytona Beach, Florida. In his book, *Glory Days: When Horsepower and Passion Ruled Detroit,* Wangers states, "One of the best promotions we ever put together was our first one, with *Car and Driver*. We agreed to supply two Pontiac GTOs, one a stock Sports Coupe with standard suspension, a 348-hp Tri-Power engine, a wide-ratio 4-speed gearbox, and a limited-slip

This 1964 GTO convertible, equipped with an automatic transmission, is similar to the one tested in the December 1963 issue of *Hot Rod* magazine. Heavier than the hardtop versions and lacking a manual transmission, it wasn't the ideal model for a high-profile performance road test.

Featured in the March 1964 issue, the famous Grenadier Red 1964 GTO was one of two cars used during the *Car and Driver* tests in Daytona, Florida. A line from the article read, "One expects the acceleration to be spectacular in first and second, but none of us were ready for the awful slamming back in the seat we got when we tromped on it at 80 in fourth." (Photo Courtesy Don Keefe)

3.55:1 rear end. The second GTO, which became known as the "red car" because it was painted Grenadier Red, also had the 348 Tri-Power engine but used a close-ratio 4-speed and a 3.90:1 limited slip rear end."

Although a Ferrari GTO never actually participated in the experiment, it was still a triumph for Wangers, as both Pontiacs performed admirably and the "red car" absolutely stunned the editors from *Car and Driver* with its brute force. Many automotive critics suspected that the results of the *Car and Driver* tests could not possibly be accurate, or that there was more than a well-tuned 389-ci engine under the hood of the red GTO.

In *Glory Days*, Wangers confesses, "I'm here to admit, more than three decades after the fact, that yes, I did install a 421 H.O. Tri-Power engine in the red Royal Bobcat *Car and Driver* test car."

Jim Wangers' involvement with the Pontiac GTO extended well beyond its debut year, including the creation of many campaigns that have since become synonymous with Pontiac performance. Among them was the outrageous tiger theme, which used live tigers in many television and print ads. His style and techniques are some of the most revered and imitated in the automotive industry. When asked if he feels that Dodge is employing similar, performance-oriented marketing, he replied enthusiastically, "Hell yeah! They're almost copying what we did, but more power to them. They are

doing it very effectively, too. I met a few of those guys; great people with a positive attitude."

At more than 90 years old, Jim Wangers remains passionate about all things automotive and could be considered the ultimate G.O.A.T. (greatest of all time).

The Royal Pontiac–prepped 421 H.O. engine is virtually indistinguishable from a factory-issued 389-ci unit. When asked why he ordered the 421-ci to be installed in the *Car and Driver* test car, Wangers replied, "When you go to a picnic, you always bring your best ingredients." Indeed, the 421 H.O. was Pontiac's top engine at the time and is still considered by many enthusiasts to be the epitome of a Pontiac street engine. The custom air cleaner was designed by Milt Schornack and was likely added soon after the *Car and Driver* tests. (Photo Courtesy Don Keefe)

Pontiac's use of the GTO name irritated certain sports car purists. They felt that an American car was unworthy of the name that was already being used by Italian carmaker Ferrari.

Bunkie Knudsen had brought Pontiac Motor Division back into relevance by producing innovative and exciting automobiles, but the GM racing ban in 1963 threatened to derail the performance image that Knudsen, along with Pete Estes and John DeLorean, had tirelessly promoted since 1957. Applying their knowledge of racing programs from the late 1950s and early 1960s to production cars, the management team at Pontiac created what became one of the most iconic American cars of all time.

Choosing the name GTO was a bold and daring move by John DeLorean, as it was already being used by Ferrari on one of the most exotic and high-performing automobiles ever constructed, the Ferrari 250 GTO. In Italian, GTO stands for *Gran Tur-*

ismo Omologato, which translates to Grand Touring Homologated. That term simply means a manufacturer has produced at least 100 cars to compete in the Grand Touring class of international road racing. Interestingly, Ferrari did not produce enough GTOs to officially qualify for the Grand Touring series but was able to circumvent the rule by numbering the chassis out of sequence, thereby giving the impression that more cars were produced than was actually the case.

Another obstacle for DeLorean and his crew was that General Motors had a strict policy stating that no intermediate car could have an engine over 330 ci. The clever team at Pontiac was able to sidestep this regulation by offering the GTO as an option for the LeMans, and not as a separate model. Once again, DeLorean and Wangers were pushing the boundaries of what could be accomplished within the tight framework of General Motors.

TEMPEST STANDARD EQUIPMENT

In 1964, the newly redesigned Pontiac Tempest and LeMans lineup was well received by the automotive press and the general public. The 4-cylinder engine, torque tube, and rear-mounted transaxle were elimi- nated on the 1964 models and replaced with a more conventional front-mounted engine and transmission layout. Attractive new sheet metal, combined with various engine options and body configurations, resulted in strong sales of 202,676 units.

A 215-ci inline 6-cylinder, topped with a 1-barrel carburetor that put out 140 hp, was the standard Tempest engine. Two versions of the 326-ci V-8 were offered as options, including a 280-hp 4-barrel version. This 326 H.O. engine was a competent performer and foreshadowed the

Standard Tempest wheels measured 14 x 5 inches, quite small by today's standards. While "dog dish" hubcaps were standard, this Tempest displays the optional Deluxe wheel covers.

Simple yet tasteful, the interior space of the 1964 Tempest and LeMans models are similar to that of the GTO. Note the color-keyed standard steering wheel, the same one included in the GTO package unless the optional Custom Sports wheel was specified.

At a quick glance, this 1964 Pontiac Tempest Custom could easily be mistaken for a 1964 GTO. A closer inspection reveals the exterior differences. The Tempest Custom featured additional trim on the sides, and unlike the GTO, it did not have hood scoops.

yet-to-be released GTO option. A 3-speed column-shifted manual transmission was standard with an optional 2-speed automatic or an optional 4-speed manual.

Standard wheels for the 1964 Tempest measured 14 x 5 inches and were adorned with small "dog-dish" hubcaps, with full wheel covers available at extra cost. Tires were 6.5 inches wide and consisted of a bias-ply construction, which was common for this time period.

The cabins of the 1964 Tempests were thoughtfully styled but minimally appointed and featured a front bench seat (although bucket seats were available on the LeMans and standard on the GTO). Smaller items, such as doorjamb light switches, passenger-side sun visors, and cigarette lighters, which were optional equipment or not available on previous years, became standard on the 1964 Tempest models.

GTO EQUIPMENT PACKAGE

For $295.90 (approximately $2,283 today), the GTO option (RPO 382) consisted of a 389-ci engine fed by a single 4-barrel carburetor, backed by a 3-speed manual transmission with a heavy-duty 10.4-inch-diameter clutch and a Hurst shifter. Various suspension upgrades, dual exhaust, and a 3.23:1 axle ratio were also standard equipment when the GTO option was specified. Twin hood scoops, various GTO callouts, and a distinctive taillight panel (shared only with the LeMans) were part of the GTO package. An engine-turned dash appliqué and bucket seats for the interior set it further apart from other 1964 Tempest models.

Available Bodies

The 1964 Pontiac GTO was available in three configurations: convertible, two-door hardtop, and two-door sedan, which Pontiac called "Sports Coupe." Unlike the Tempest models, the GTO was not available as a four-door sedan or four-door station wagon, which further emphasized the performance motif.

With 18,422 units produced, the two-door hardtop (style 37) was by far the most popular version. On these cars, when the door and quarter windows are lowered, there is no visible structure, and the result is very clean and unobstructed. Four horizontally mounted headlights were used in all Tempest, LeMans, and GTO models for 1964. Although attractive, it was a departure from

Debuting in late 1963, the 1964 Pontiac GTO was a stunningly attractive automobile. This Marimba Red Sports Coupe features a Parchment interior, redline tires, and Custom wheel covers.

Despite it being the final body type into production, hardtop numbers reached 18,422 units in 1964, more than the Sports Coupe and convertible combined. Production for the hardtop jumped to 55,722 for the 1965 model year, providing further evidence that the GTO was a winner.

The Sports Coupe shared many of the same lines as the hardtop examples, but with only 7,384 Sports Coupes produced in 1964, they are highly collectible. Even when the door window is lowered, the steel frame and trim are still visible.

Perfect for cruising day or night, the 1964 GTO convertible was the rarest of the three body styles, with just 6,644 being produced. By 1966, that number nearly doubled when Pontiac manufactured 12,798 GTO convertibles.

other Pontiac automobiles of that year, which featured a stacked headlight design that the GTO acquired from 1965 to 1967. Although strong arguments could be made for other model years (1965 and 1970 in particular), the 1964 two-door hardtop is considered by many Pontiac devotees to be the quintessential GTO.

Upon first glance, the two-door Sports Coupe (style 27) appears similar to the hardtop, but a structural B-pillar, or "post," separates the door and quarter area and features a steel window frame, which remains visible even when the window is lowered. This results in a somewhat cluttered look, but also the greatest structural rigidity and lightest weight of the three body styles. The Sports Coupe was a favorite among racers, most notably, Arnie Beswick and his *Mystery Tornado* drag car.

Only 7,384 two-door Sports Coupes were built in 1964, making them highly collectible, especially when equipped with some of the more desired options,

such as Tri-Power induction and 4-speed manual transmission.

While some 1964 GTO convertibles were built with high-performance upgrades, they generally appealed to a slightly different automotive enthusiast, one that preferred drive-in movies and cruising the boulevard, not wringing out every last MPH at the dragstrip. Pontiac produced 6,644 GTO convertibles (style 67) in 1964, making them the rarest of the three configurations, and often, the most valuable.

The boxed frame rails of the convertibles, along with other reinforcements made to the body and frame, resulted in the convertible being the heaviest of the three body types. It should be noted that convertibles of all makes, not just Pontiacs, were typically heavier than other body styles offered. A heavy-duty frame option for the hardtop or Sports Coupe bodies was available, which used the stronger, convertible boxed frame.

Marketing the GTO

Arriving in October/November 1963, the GTO was a late addition to the 1964 Pontiac lineup. With this timing, combined with GM upper management apprehensiveness about the car, initial advertising was modest, and even restrained compared to what it soon became.

In a dealer training film on the 1964 Tempest and LeMans series, the GTO was only given brief mention,

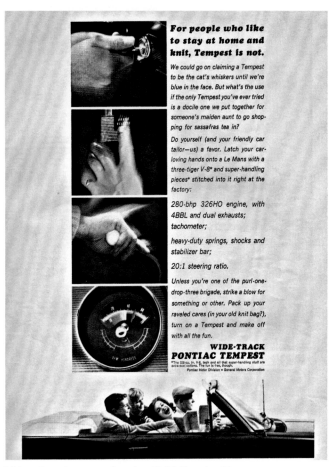

For people who like to stay at home and knit, Tempest is not.

We could go on claiming a Tempest to be the cat's whiskers until we're blue in the face. But what's the use if the only Tempest you've ever tried is a docile one we put together for someone's maiden aunt to go shopping for sassafras tea in?

Do yourself (and your friendly car tailor—us) a favor. Latch your car-loving hands onto a Le Mans with a three-tiger V-8* and super-handling pieces* stitched into it right at the factory:

280-bhp 326HO engine, with 4BBL and dual exhausts;

tachometer;

heavy-duty springs, shocks and stabilizer bar;

20:1 steering ratio.

Unless you're one of the purl-one-drop-three brigade, strike a blow for something or other. Pack up your raveled cares (in your old knit bag?), turn on a Tempest and make off with all the fun.

WIDE-TRACK PONTIAC TEMPEST

*The 326-cu. in. V-8, tach and all that super-handling stuff are extra-cost options. The fun is free, though.
Pontiac Motor Division • General Motors Corporation

This advertisement for the 1963 Pontiac Tempest foreshadowed the performance-based youth-oriented advertisements that were developed for the 1964 GTO. The ad is also one of Pontiac's first use of a tiger reference, as it refers to the 280-hp 326-ci engine as a "three tiger V-8." (Photo Courtesy GM Media Archive)

and the narrator simply boasted, "The styling and engineering features of this option result in the finest rally-type American production car available." Many details of the GTO were not disclosed, and the overall emphasis appeared to be merely informing salesmen of the available body configurations for the 1964 model year, not the performance characteristics of the new GTO option.

Another dealer instructional film for the 1964 Pontiacs went into great detail on the new Tempest and LeMans models, even touting the performance of the 280-hp 326-ci V-8 engine. However, the GTO was conspicuously absent. This was likely due to the fact that the film was produced in early to mid-1963 and the GTO was still in development and planning stages.

It's interesting to note that Pontiac was emphasizing a smooth and quiet ride quality, a theme that was repeated throughout the duration of the film, with the narrator stating, "The Pontiac is not just a little bit quieter and smoother than other makes, it's very noticeably quieter and easier riding." Those are perhaps two aspects that the performance-minded enthusiast would not consider to be positive characteristics.

General Motors initially projected that just 5,000 1964 GTOs would be sold, but total production for 1964 resulted in 32,450 units, proving that DeLorean and Wangers had their fingers on the pulse of the young car-buying public. The advertising campaign for the Pontiac GTO eventually became enthusiastic and aggressive, portraying the car as a powerful and desirable machine coveted by the trendsetting youth of America. Its renegade image was heavily promoted in magazines, on television, and at live events across the nation.

Pontiac first used the tiger theme in an advertisement for the 1963 Tempest. Depicting two cars, one with the 4-cylinder engine and the other with the new 260-hp 326-ci V-8, it asked, "Can you tell which Tempest is the tiger?" Another print advertisement for the 1963 Tempest features four young people in a Tempest convertible accompanied by four action photos with a layout that is quite similar to the GTO ads that soon

GTO is for kicking up the kind of storm that others just talk up.

Standard Equipment: engine: 389-cu. in. Pontiac with 1-4BBL; bhp—325 @ 4800; torque—428 lb-ft @ 3200 rpm/dual-exhaust system/3-speed stick with Hurst shifter/heavy-duty clutch/ heavy-duty springs, shocks, stabilizer bar/special 7.50 x 14 red-line high-speed nylon cord tires (rayon cord whitewalls optional at no extra cost/14 x 6JK wide-rim wheels/high-capacity radiator / declutching fan / high-capacity battery (66 plate, 61 amp. hr.)/chromed air cleaner, rocker covers, oil filler cap/bucket seats/standard axle ratio 3.23:1 (3.08, 3.36*, 3.55* to 1 available on special order at no extra cost. And some of our extra-cost Performance Options: engine: 389-cu. in. Pontiac with 3-2BBL (Code #809); bhp—348 @ 4900;
*Available only with heavy-duty options at slight additional charge.

torque—428 lb-ft @ 3600; 3.55:1 axle ratio standard with this engine option/4-speed with Hurst shifter (gear ratios 2.56:1, 1.91:1, 1.48:1, 1.00:1, and 2.64:1 reverse)/2-speed automatic with 2.20:1 torque converter/Safe-T-Track limited-slip differ-ential (Code #701)/3.90:1 axle ratio available on special order with metallic brake linings, heavy-duty radiator and Safe-T-Track/handling kit—20:1 quick steering and extra-firm-control heavy-duty shocks (Code #612)/high-performance full tran-sistor (breakerless) ignition (Code #671)/tachometer (Code #452)/custom sports steering wheel (Code #524)/exhaust splitters (Dealer installed)/wire wheel discs (Dealer installed)/ custom wheel discs, with spinner and brake cooling holes (Code #521)/console (Code #601).

the GTO makers—Pontiac
PONTIAC MOTOR DIVISION • GENERAL MOTORS CORPORATION

An early print ad for the 1964 GTO. Four action photos accompanied by a detailed list of performance equipment provided a simple, yet effective way of marketing Pontiac's new high-performance model. (Photo Courtesy GM Media Archive)

followed. The text is aggressive, challenging the poten-tial buyer to purchase this high-performance machine and, "Turn on a Tempest and make off with all the fun."

Esso and Uniroyal were also using tiger imagery to promote their products, with Esso stating, "Put a tiger in your tank!" In Jim Wangers' book, *Glory Days*, he recalls, "When U.S. Royal approached us about using their new 'Tiger Paw' on every new GTO, the opportunity for an advertising tie-in was a natural. We had already con-

For the man who wouldn't mind riding a tiger if someone'd only put wheels on it—Pontiac GTO

This piece of machinery is something our Engineering Depart-ment slipped a motherly big Pontiac 389-incher into and named the GTO.

It comes in hardtop, sports coupe and convertible form, based on the Le Mans—only sleekened down some and fitted with a special set of red-circle high-performance tires.

The looks you can see for yourself. The big deal is under the hood: 325 bhp at 4800 rpm and 428 lb-ft of torque at 3200 rpm. That's just the standard 4BBL engine. There's also a version with 348 bhp* at 4900 rpm and 428 lb-ft of torque at 3600 rpm.
*optional at extra cost.

This one does deep-breathing exercises through a 3-2BBL setup. Both make bad-tempered noises through dual pipes. As illustrated above, pairs of exhaust splitters on each flank, just behind the rear wheels, are available dealer installed*.

A 3-speed transmission is standard, stirred by a Hurst shifter on the floor. Extra-cost variations include an automatic with shift on the column . . . an all-synchro 4-speed on the floor . . . or a choice of any one of them sprouting out of a console.

Give yourself a blast of tonic. Sample one of these here big pussycats.
PONTIAC MOTOR DIVISION • GENERAL MOTORS CORPORATION

Tempest Ad No. T64-1030
1 page—7 x 10 inches—B&W
Motor Trend—December, 1963
Car Life—December, 1963
Hot Rod—December, 1963
Car & Driver—December, 1963
Road & Track—December, 1963
(A) Mechanix Illustrated—December, 1963
(A) Popular Science Monthly—December, 1963
(A) Popular Mechanics—December, 1963
MacMANUS, JOHN & ADAMS, Inc.
26817—W-F—9-26-63 (98)

This now-famous advertisement for the 1964 GTO achieved exactly what Jim Wangers set out to accomplish, reaching directly to the performance market. Displaying the 4-barrel carburetor, manual transmission shifter, and the car at speed, there was no mistaking what the GTO was built for. (Photo Courtesy GM Media Archive)

sidered using the tiger theme for the GTO, since it had been used in some 1963 Tempest/LeMans advertising." Some Pontiac historians opine that the Tiger Paw tires were chosen at least partially for their ability to quickly spin and produce clouds of tire smoke, further portray-ing the GTO as an untamable street beast.

Pontiac dealerships distributed bold "GR-RRR!" license plates as a fun and clever way to market the GTO's aggressive attitude. Pontiac collectors covet original vintage examples. This piece is proudly affixed to a 1968 model.

With limited time and resources, Jim Wangers suggested that early GTO advertisements be placed in automotive magazines such as *Hot Rod* and *Car Craft*, figuring that Pontiac could directly reach the type of potential buyer for which the GTO was built without raising too many eyebrows at the top executive level. Wangers recalls, "I always seemed to be fighting an uphill battle with upper management. They seemed to be afraid of what we wanted to do; it was all so new to them."

One clever print ad from this period bragged, "GTO is for kicking up the kind of storm that others just talk up." It featured various photos of gearslamming and spinning tires accompanied by text that simply listed the standard and optional performance equipment. It was a perfect example of what Wangers and the rest of Pontiac's marketing team were trying to accomplish: Promote the GTO directly to the performance-minded car buyer within the constraints set by the conservative upper management at General Motors.

Another early print ad for the GTO depicts its various performance components and a photo of the car

Pontiac successfully used the tiger marketing theme through the 1966 model year. Novelty items, including the tiger tail, were yet another way that the tiger image was used in the promotion of the GTO.

at speed with the line, "For the man who wouldn't mind riding a tiger if someone'd only put wheels on it—Pontiac GTO." It was one of the first instances where the tiger theme was used to promote the GTO, and soon, tiger imagery became synonymous with the car. Various promotional items, such as tiger tails and license plates, were made available to the Pontiac enthusiast.

Pontiac's performance advertising soon began to include the full-size models within the brand, building upon the early success of the GTO. One such ad from 1964 displayed a photo of an empty garage at night with the line, "There's a tiger loose in the streets." There was no photo of the car or its components, which only added to the mystique. The text described an exciting late-night drive and ended with, "Have you tried one of our 421s?"

The GTO was rapidly becoming a cultural phenomenon, and rock bands were soon singing the praises of Pontiac's hot new car. Surf-rock band Ronny and the Daytonas scored a number-four hit with their song, "G.T.O." Released in January 1964 and featuring lyrics such as "Three deuces and a four speed and a 389," it was set to an energetic rhythm and showcased soaring vocals. It was the perfect song to further hype Pontiac's new performance model. Similarly, popular surf-rock duo Jan and Dean released "My Mighty GTO" in June 1964, which bragged, "On the way to the strip, ya know she shows lots of style, but nobody takes her in the quarter-mile."

In May 1965, Pontiac got in on the action when Jim Wangers helped assemble the band The Tigers. The song "GeeTO Tiger" was not as popular as earlier efforts performed by more established acts, but due to its relative obscurity, the album is now a highly collectible piece of early GTO history. The opposite side of the record was called Big Sounds of the GeeTO Tiger and featured authentic 1964 GTO engine sounds accompanied by voices to narrate the experience. Early on, a man warns, "You'd better use your belt. We're gonna do some pretty tough testing."

The event was initially to be recorded at the GM Proving Grounds, but according to Jim Wangers, scheduling conflicts forced the project to be recorded at a dragstrip in California's San Fernando Valley. Final touches, such as additional voices and sound effects, were added later at a studio in Hollywood.

By the time the first GTO television commercial appeared in 1965, Pontiac's marketing strategies were hard hitting and assertive. A scene opened with a menacing tiger on the prowl that then jumped into the engine compartment of a 1965 GTO. Actor William Conrad implored buyers, "Go price one, one of the Wide-Track tigers from Pontiac." In late 1966, the tiger theme was discontinued, as it was deemed too aggressive by GM upper management.

The marketing gurus at Pontiac later developed a number of memorable advertising strategies for the GTO and other models within the brand. "The Great One" campaign, which debuted for the 1967 GTO, was also used in a print ad for the restyled 1968 model and boasted the lines, "There's only one Great One. We've been proving it for five years."

When the GTO Judge was unveiled in 1969, it presented Pontiac advertising executives with a new hook for marketing. Judge and courtroom scenarios soon permeated print publications and television commercials. The Judge name was pulled from the trendy comedy television series, Rowan and Martin's Laugh-In. In a popular skit, Sammy Davis Jr. was adorned in judge attire and repeated the phrase, "Here come da judge, here come da judge!" It was a clever bit of marketing that further heightened Pontiac's pop culture presence.

From late 1964 to 1970, the various advertising campaigns for the Pontiac GTO, along with inclusions in television, movies, and popular music, became some of the most memorable in automotive history. Such promotions greatly enhanced the youth-oriented image that was being cultivated by the creative experts within Pontiac Motor Division.

The appeal of the 1964 Pontiac GTO is obvious. This triple black convertible features Hurst wheels, Tri-Power, and 4-speed transmission. The Hurst wheels debuted in 1965 and were aftermarket-only components but look great on this Starlight Black 1964 model.

CHAPTER 3

ENGINE, TRANSMISSION AND REAR END

The base engine for the 1964 Pontiac GTO was a 389-ci powerplant fed by a 4-barrel Carter carburetor. This configuration was rated at 325 hp at 4,800 rpm and 428 ft-lbs of torque at just 3,200 rpm, making it an ideal street engine.

Pontiac's overhead-valve V-8 engine debuted in 1955 with 287 ci, and by increasing the bore and stroke, it grew in displacement each year until it reached 389 ci in 1959. The 389-ci was a reliable and versatile engine for Pontiac until the 400-ci replaced it in 1967. The 400-ci was achieved simply by increasing the bore of the popular 389-ci from 4.0625 inches to 4.12 and was a solid performer for more than a decade, until the last units were installed in 1979.

389 ENGINE

The Pontiac 389-ci engine displayed a 4.0625-inch bore and a 3.75-inch stroke, and through various improvements made since its debut in 1959, such as cylinder head and camshaft design, it became a high-performing powerplant. For the 1964 GTO, engineers made further advancements, transforming the 389-ci into the ideal engine for Pontiac's hot new street car.

The cylinder head casting number is located on the center exhaust ports. The 9770716 heads were first used on the 1963 421 H.O. engines in some of Pontiac's full-size performance cars.

As in other cars from the era, the 389-ci powerplant in the 1964 GTO employed an engine block made from cast iron. An Arma-Steel crankshaft was fitted to the block and featured 3.00-inch mains secured by two-bolt main bearing caps. Connecting rods measured 6.625 inches and were also constructed from Arma-Steel. Although technically not steel, Arma-Steel is the GM trade name for a type of durable cast iron and was used in numerous applications for many years.

Pistons were cast-aluminum units and were reliable in all but the most extreme conditions. Pontiac's Super Duty engines employed forged aluminum pistons for the added durability needed for racing applications.

High-flowing, efficient cylinder heads are crucial to an engine's overall performance. Pontiac engineers chose casting number 9770716 (often referred to as 716) cylinder heads for the 389-ci engine in the 1964 GTO. These were the same units on the 421 H.O. engines housed in some of Pontiac's full-size performance cars and featured 1.92-inch intake and 1.66-inch exhaust valves, in contrast to the smaller 1.88- and 1.60-inch valves found in Pontiac's lower-performing V-8 engines. These heads also featured larger intake and exhaust

Some enthusiasts felt that the 500-cfm Carter carburetor was too small for the large, powerful 389-ci engine. Nevertheless, it performed admirably and, for most gearheads, was easier to tune than the Tri-Power induction system. (Photo Courtesy Andre Rayman)

ports than the standard 389-ci engines, which, when combined with the larger valves, allowed for more air and fuel, resulting in additional power. The 68-cc combustion chamber of these cylinder heads, along with the flat-top pistons, yielded a compression ratio of 10.75:1.

The camshaft design, in conjunction with cylinder head efficiency, is perhaps the most critical element of any engine. The camshaft operates the valves and controls how *long* they stay open (known as camshaft duration) and how *far* they open (known as valve lift). The camshaft profile greatly affects horsepower, torque, RPM potential, and even fuel economy. The engineers at Pontiac fitted the GTO's 389-ci with a hydraulic-lifter camshaft that displayed 273 intake/289 exhaust degrees of duration and a .407-inch valve lift when used with the factory-issued 1.5:1 rocker arms.

Pontiac V-8 engines had the distributor mounted in the rear center position of the block. The external coil was located along the back of the passenger-side cylinder head.

The exhaust on the 1964 GTO was a true dual system, exiting just behind each rear wheel. Chrome-plated tailpipe extensions (code 422), often referred to as splitters, were a $21.30 option for the 1964 model and added some flair to the rear of the car.

The hydraulic lifters used in the 1964 GTO were an improvement over the units installed in standard 389-ci engines. These lifters featured a unique internal design that consisted of a small check-valve that, when combined with the heavy-duty valvesprings, increased the engine's high-RPM capability. However, research suggests that the 389-ci engines for use in the GTO built prior to mid-November 1963 may not have been equipped with the heavy-duty valvesprings, even though all GTO engines produced after November 1963 did receive the stiffer valvesprings.

In addition, Pontiac V-8 engines equipped with the 9770716 cylinder heads used an oiling system that employed hollow pushrods and redesigned rocker arms to provide oil to the upper part of the valvetrain. The previous design (including other 1964 Pontiac V-8 engines) used hollow rocker arm studs that made them prone to failure in high-horsepower applications. Beginning in 1965, Pontiac adopted the new oiling system throughout its engine lineup, eliminating the hollow rocker arm studs.

The standard induction system on the 1964 GTO consisted of a single 500-cfm Carter AFB 4-barrel carburetor mounted on a dual-plane cast-iron intake manifold. The Carter AFB featured 1.438-inch primary and slightly larger 1.688-inch secondary throttle bores, and while it performed admirably, many Pontiac enthusiasts felt that the Carter carburetor was too small for the large, powerful 389-ci engine in the GTO. The 4-barrel GTOs were topped with a chrome-plated single-snorkel air cleaner that was unique to the 1964 model. Chrome valvecovers complemented the air cleaner and provided the owner yet another reason to show off the engine.

The air/fuel mixture was sparked by a common points-style distributor with a transistor ignition (code 671) available as a $75.27 option, quite a large sum in 1964. The spent fumes exited via common exhaust manifolds into a true dual system that was standard equipment for the GTO package. In addition to increasing power, the macho tone emanating from the pipes was likely a key ingredient to the GTO's success.

The standard combination was rated at 325 hp and 428 ft-lbs of torque and the potent engine certainly impressed many writers in the automotive press. In the January 1964 issue of *Motor Trend*, writer Bob McVay stated, "Our first and lasting impression of the Tempest (GTO) was one of more-than-adequate power; our first acceleration run left our photographer standing in a huge cloud of blue rubber smoke, looking at a long black strip on the pavement."

TRI-POWER

Although Pontiac's Tri-Power induction system had been available since 1957, the 1964 GTO further popularized the option and the Tri-Power has since become synonymous with early GTO models. This induction setup featured three Rochester 2-barrel carburetors

atop a cast-iron intake manifold that employed vacuum linkage to operate the two outboard carburetors. Due to the additional air and fuel it provided over the 4-barrel, horsepower increased from 325 to 348 hp.

The Tri-Power system was not without its peculiarities; under normal driving conditions, the engine was fed solely by the center carburetor, but when the vacuum signal reached a certain point, both outboard carburetors opened fully and a surge of acceleration occurred. Depending upon the owner's driving habits, this could be viewed negatively or positively. In addition, due to remaining vacuum in the lines, the outboard carburetors could stay open momentarily, even after lifting off the accelerator.

Mechanical linkage became available later in the 1964 model year as an over-the-counter item and

Pontiac's Tri-Power induction system had been available since 1957, when it debuted on the 347-ci engine. The 389-ci Tri-Power engine in the 1964 GTO was rated at 348 hp at 4,900 rpm and 428 ft-lbs of torque at 3,600 rpm. It is interesting to note that the torque output for both the 4-barrel and Tri-Power cars were the same, just at different RPM.

In this highly detailed 1964 Tri-Power setup, the factory-correct foam air cleaner elements, along with proper lettering stamped on the hoses and handwritten numbers on the carburetors, helped this GTO win numerous awards. However, with the 1964 GTO being produced at four different facilities, assembly markings can vary from plant to plant.

The 1966 model was the last year for the Tri-Power induction setup in the GTO. From 1967 through 1974, the Rochester Quadrajet 4-barrel carburetor performed admirably and offered a combination of fuel economy and performance.

provided a more controlled, smoother transition from part throttle to full throttle. A competent GTO owner could install the new linkage or choose to have a local Pontiac dealership make the conversion.

In addition to increased power, the Tri-Power system had the benefit of being visually impressive, and GTO owners took great pride in popping the hood to show off the induction system. The Tri-Power featured three small chrome-plated air cleaners with black foam filtration elements. Although stylish, the small air cleaners were more restrictive than the larger units installed on other performance cars of the era.

Because the Tri-Power has become so closely associated with the 1964 GTO, it's interesting to note that far more cars were factory equipped with the standard 4-barrel intake and Carter AFB carburetor: 24,205 with the 4-barrel and only 8,245 with Tri-Power. Today, many GTO owners consider the Tri-Power essential equipment for the 1964 model and have converted their factory 4-barrel cars to the Tri-Power arrangement, even on restored examples.

Tri-Power was available on the GTO through the 1966 model year, after which General Motors decided that multiple carburetion was only to be used on its flagship sports car, the Chevrolet Corvette. In addition, 1966 was the last year for GTOs equipped with the Carter AFB carburetor, replaced by the larger Rochester Quadrajet in 1967. Vastly different than the Carter AFB, the Quadrajet featured small 1.38-inch primary throttle bores and huge 2.25-inch secondary bores. This arrangement offered good fuel economy when driven with restraint and plenty of power when the large secondaries opened.

Chrome valvecovers were standard equipment on all GTOs until the 1971 model year, which received painted pieces in the same hue as the engine. This practice lasted through the 1974 production run.

Period correct battery complete with "spring ring" battery cables. The standard battery was the Delco DC-12; the heavy-duty version was Delco DC-250. The heavy-duty battery (code 582) was a $3.55 option and was installed in all cars equipped with air conditioning.

Although many Pontiac fans were disappointed by the discontinuation of the Tri-Power setup, the 400-ci engine topped with the Rochester Quadrajet carburetor was a solid performer for 1967 and beyond.

The GTO's 389-ci engine clearly displayed large amounts of low- and mid-range power, and owners soon discovered that their new car was ideal for stoplight-to-stoplight street racing. Further tuning techniques performed by savvy gearheads, such as ignition timing and carburetor adjustments, extracted even more power from the 389-ci, and the 1964 GTO soon became a legend.

TRANSMISSIONS

Four transmission choices were available for the 1964 GTO, including the M21 close-ratio 4-speed, which arrived late in the model year. The Muncie 3-speed manual transmission was standard. This unit featured a 2.58 first gear, 1.48 second, and 1:1 third gear. Although adequate, it didn't quite possess the true gear-slamming experience that the 4-speed provided, and many GTO owners eventually converted their cars to 4-speed units.

A popular factory option for the GTO was the Muncie M20 wide-ratio 4-speed manual transmission. The addition of the extra gear facilitated better acceleration and, when taking corners, enabled the driver to choose a gear that kept the engine RPM near the peak power range. Gear ratios for the 4-speed were 2.56 in first, 1.91 in second, 1.48 in third, and 1:1 in fourth. A heavy-duty clutch was employed for the 3- and 4-speed manual transmissions.

Another 4-speed manual transmission, the Muncie M21 close-ratio, was made available late in the 1964 model year. This transmission featured gear ratios of 2.20 in first, 1.64 in second, 1.25:1 in third, and 1:1 in fourth. Due to the late availability and complexities in the ordering process, 1964 Pontiac GTOs factory issued with the M21 close-ratio are extremely rare and valuable.

Respected 1964 GTO hobbyist John Viale has conducted countless hours of research to unravel a topic that, to many Pontiac enthusiasts, has remained shrouded in mystery. His explanation follows:

The speedometer drive gear (internal to the Muncie 4-speed) needed for all Tempest applications, including the GTO, was an eight-tooth piece, with the only exception being if the order called for the 3.90:1 axle ratio. In that case, the speedometer drive gear needed to be a six-tooth unit. Because the speedometer drive gear was part of the transmission assembly, Pontiac needed Muncie to produce two specific versions of the wide-ratio M20: one for use with all applications except the 3.90 axle and one for use with the 3.90 axle.

Pontiac assigned part number 9774825 to the transmission assembly needed for all applications, except the 3.90 axle with the transmission code W, derived from sales code 77W. Part number 9774826 was assigned to the transmission assembly needed for all applications with the 3.90 axle, along with transmission code 9, drawn from sales code 779; this transmission was identical to the code W except for the internal speedometer drive gear. The buyer never ordered this transmission specifically; he or she ordered the 4-speed option. The selection of one or the other was simply a consequence of the axle ratio being installed.

The M21 close-ratio was not available at the beginning of GTO production and was first mentioned in the second version of the GTO sales brochure dated April 17, 1964. It was assigned part number 9777000, with sales code 778 and transmission code 8. It featured a six-tooth internal speedometer drive gear like the code 9 M20. (Incidentally, the part numbers were embossed on a small metal tag and bolted to the side cover.)

To order the M21 transmission, Pontiac made several option components mandatory, which contributed to its limited production. The GTO package, Tri-Power, and 3.90 axle all had to be specified. The additional features that normally accompanied the 3.90 axle were also required and included metallic brake linings, Safe-T-Track rear end, heavy-duty fan, and heavy-duty radiator. The buyer did not have to order the close-ratio M21 to get the 3.90 axle. Until the M21 was released, you could order the 3.90 and 4-speed and receive the code 9 wide-ratio M20. The buyer could still order it that way after the M21 became available.

Further complicating matters was the now-famous March 1964 *Car and Driver* article, which claimed that the 4-speeds in the two GTOs tested were Muncie units, stating, "It had the new GM Muncie 4-speed transmission." In the article, the magazine listed the transmission gear ratios; they are not Muncie M21 ratios, but rather BorgWarner ratios. Whatever the reason for the misinformation, that article spurred numerous sales of 3.90-axle GTOs built in March. Many buyers thought they were getting a close-ratio M21 because of what they read in *Car and Driver*; instead they received the code 9 M20, as the M21 was yet to be released.

Even today, many GTO enthusiasts believe that ordering the 3.90:1 axle ratio got you the close-ratio M21 (that and the fact that PHS still asserts that the code 9 is a close-ratio based on the old, erroneous published material). Whenever the original transmissions have been studied, they have always been found to be part number 9774826, code 9, M20 wide-ratio units, exactly as Pontiac Motor Division intended them to be.

To date, no 1964 GTO is known to still exist that was built with the M21. John Viale states, "I am aware of one, but the car is gone; however, the VIN-matched original transmission does still exist along with the original tattered window sticker for the car. As a Fremont build, the window sticker not only identifies the trans as an M21, but also lists the sales code 778. Fremont 1964 Window Stickers listed options by Universal Production Code (UPC) (M21 is a UPC) and Sales Code (778 in this case)."

Thanks to Viale's comprehensive research, in conjunction with input from other notable 1964 GTO experts, this description of the coding and availability of the M21 close-ratio 4-speed transmission is the most detailed and current available.

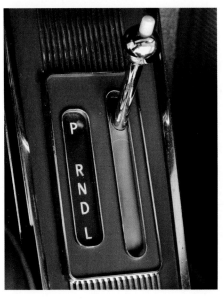

The 2-speed automatic shifter appeared in the optional console. Cars equipped with the automatic transmission and no console had the shifter mounted on the steering column. This didn't exactly befit the GTO's high-performance image.

the large 389-ci engine, compared with a 2.5:1 ratio for the 326-ci Tempest and LeMans.

Because it is a GM 2-speed automatic transmission, many hobbyists wrongly assume that the Super Turbine 300 is closely related to Chevrolet's Powerglide transmission, when, in fact, very few similarities exist between the two. The Super Turbine 300 automatic transmission was not as popular as the manual versions and was better suited to leisurely cruising than spirited performance driving. It did, however, provide the potential buyer who was not accustomed to manual shifting the ability to purchase a GTO.

HURST SHIFTER

Jim Wangers had extensive drag racing experience, and he knew which components that performance enthusiasts required on a car such as the GTO. He lobbied to have a Hurst shifter issued as standard equipment on both the 3- and 4-speed manual transmissions.

An excerpt from the March 1964 issue of *Car and Driver* stated, "The transmission lever is nicely placed immediately next to the driver's thigh. It has the now famous Hurst linkage, which is amazingly short and unerringly accurate . . . the brutal simplicity of that great tree trunk of a lever begins to reassure you and you start throwing shifts with the same slam-bang abandon as the drag racing types." This was precisely the type of review that Wangers and crew were hoping for with the addition of the Hurst shifter.

A 2-speed Super Turbine 300 automatic transmission was also offered in 1964 and could be ordered with the shifter mounted on the steering column or housed in the console, if equipped. Featuring a 1.76 first gear and a 1:1 second gear, the Super Turbine 300 unit installed in the 1964 GTO received a few upgrades over the standard component. A high-output governor raised the wide-open-throttle upshift to 5,200 rpm, and the forward clutch pack had six pairs of discs, compared with five for 326-ci powered Tempest and LeMans models. The torque converter's stall ratio for the GTO's Super Turbine 300 was adjusted to 2.2:1 for use behind

Although stylish, the 4-speed shifter lever adorned with the Hurst name is not correct for the 1964 GTO. An internal policy prohibited the manufacturer's name from being displayed on factory-installed aftermarket parts. However, GM executives soon realized that having the Hurst name on the shifter was an asset, and beginning in 1965, manual-transmission-equipped GTOs displayed the Hurst logo.

Despite their popularity, the shifter levers on the 1964 models did not display the Hurst name due to a GM corporate policy, but that was revised for 1965 and later years. Pontiac automobiles were frequently used in Hurst advertisements, and the partnership was beneficial to both companies. Hurst even used a scantily clad representative, Miss Hurst Golden Shifter, who helped promote the brand at automotive events across the nation.

Pat Flannery was the original Miss Hurst Golden Shifter from 1964 to 1965; she was replaced by the more familiar Linda Vaughn in late 1965. These women could be seen waving from a platform fitted to the rear of a Hurst-equipped car (usually a Pontiac or Oldsmobile) while holding onto a 9-foot-tall replica shifter.

Along with Oldsmobile, Pontiac soon became synonymous with Hurst products and, over the years, Hurst shifters and wheels have enhanced some of the most legendary muscle cars of the era.

REAR DIFFERENTIAL

The standard rear-end housing of the 1964 models used an 8.2-inch-diameter ring gear and an open differential. The rear end contained a 3.23:1 gear set as

The correct Hurst shifter without the Hurst logo protrudes proudly from the optional center console. The factory-installed Hurst units were slightly different than the versions that could be purchased at speed shops and were a combination of Hurst and Pontiac components.

The 10-bolt rear-end housing featured an 8.2-inch-diameter ring gear. This highly detailed example features a 3.90:1 axle ratio and the correct metal tag that accompanied cars equipped with the Safe-T-Track rear end.

standard equipment and 3.55 gears when the Tri-Power option was specified. However, after January 1964, Tri-power cars received 3.23 gears, although the 3.55 gears remained as optional equipment. The 3.55:1 gear

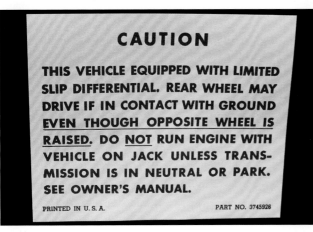

A warning decal was applied to the underside of the trunk lid for limited-slip cars. Special care was needed when servicing this type of rear end.

ratio was a good compromise between quick acceleration and highway drivability, and Pontiac reverted to this gearing as standard issue for Tri-Power cars in 1965.

Rear-end gearing was available in 3.08 to 3.90:1 ratios from the factory and 4.11 and 4.30:1 ratios as dealer-installed items. The 4.11 and 4.30 gear ratios allowed the car to accelerate much quicker from an idle and were sought after by serious drag racers of the day. The drawback to such gears was poor fuel economy and, more important, very high RPM while driving at highway speeds, which put an enormous strain on engine and transmission components.

The Safe-T-Track limited-slip differential unit was a popular performance option and an essential piece of drag racing hardware, as it effectively transferred power to both rear wheels.

Even in its basic arrangements, the 1964 Pontiac GTO was a powerful and capable automobile, and influenced an exhilarating new wave of offerings by other American manufacturers, sparking the muscle car craze.

Outward appearances could be deceptive. A mild-mannered 325-hp GTO fitted with a 2-speed automatic transmission and highway-friendly rear gears looked identical to a model equipped with the 348-hp Tri-Power option, 4-speed manual transmission, and rear-end gears that were better suited for quarter-mile drag racing than highway excursions.

CHAPTER 4

SUSPENSION AND BRAKES

Much more than a dressed-up LeMans, the 1964 Pontiac GTO had power and handling to back up its macho appearance. Burnt rubber on the pavement was a trademark of many GTO owners.

The forward-thinking engineers at Pontiac Motor Division ensured that the 1964 GTO was more than simply a Tempest with a high-output engine. The Pontiac team also provided chassis and suspension upgrades to the car, transforming it into a well-balanced performance machine. A passage from the January 1964 issue of *Motor Trend* explained, "The 389 engine isn't the only thing that makes a Tempest into a GTO. Pontiac has wisely made this a complete performance package by including such goodies as stiffer suspension with specially valved shock absorbers, a seven-blade 18-inch fan complete with cut-off clutch, dual exhaust system, special 14-inch wheels with 6-inch-wide rims (fitted with red-stripe premium nylon cord, low-profile tires), and a 10.4-inch Belleville clutch with gray-iron pressure plate for gearshift cars."

SUSPENSION

Unlike the unitized construction of previous years, the 1964 Pontiac Tempest and LeMans were built around a full-perimeter frame. Although heavier, the full-frame construction greatly increased chassis rigidity and provided a solid foundation for mounting the various suspension components. This resulted in a sturdy, more substantial automobile that also fared better in most types of collisions. The full frame, combined with the redesigned suspension, gave the 1964 units a more stable ride with enhanced road feel, superior to that of previous Tempest and LeMans models. This was also a much better configuration than the soon-to-be-released Ford Mustang, which used the Ford Falcon's unitized construction and inferior suspension.

The front suspension of the 1964 Tempest and LeMans (including the GTO) was completely different from the 1963 models. On this 1964 GTO, the lower control arm, tie-rod end, and coil spring are visibly restored to factory specifications.

A driver's-side view of where the .938-inch-diameter front sway bar attaches to the frame. The piece was standard issue for the 1964 GTO. Research suggests that the yellow paint marking is correct for a Freemont, California, build.

As on the 1964 Tempest and LeMans models, the front suspension of the GTO was an A-arm type mounted with rubber bushings. The GTO's handling was further improved by using firmer coil springs and shocks, which were standard equipment when the GTO option was specified. Likewise, the GTO came equipped with a large .938-inch front sway bar, compared to the Tempest's .875-inch unit. (Sway bars, or "anti-sway bars," control lateral movement and increase vehicle stability, especially while cornering.) A rear sway bar was not available until the 1970 model year, which was fitted with an .875-inch version. Combined with the 1.125-inch front sway bars and other redesigned suspension components, the 1970 GTO was an excellent-handling automobile. The rear suspension of the GTO was a four-link type with rubber bushings used to mount the upper and lower control arms. Like the front of the car, the rear received firmer springs and shocks. Air shocks, called the Superlift option (code 622), were also available for the rear. The Superlift option was designed more for towing than for performance, although GTO owners soon discovered they could alter the height of the rear of the car with these shocks, resulting in a more assertive appearance.

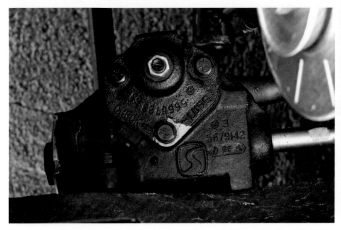

This detailed steering box is on a 1964 GTO produced at the Fremont, California, plant. Three steering ratios were offered in 1964: 24:1 manual, 20:1 optional quick ratio, and 17.5:1 for power-steering cars.

The steering box on the GTO was a Saginaw unit, with a 24:1 ratio on manual steering cars and a 17.5:1 ratio when power steering was selected. A shock absorber for the steering linkage was optional for cars with manual steering; it helped dampen vibrations to the steering wheel, providing a smoother driving experience.

"For the man who wouldn't mind riding a tiger if someone'd only put wheels on it—Pontiac GTO." The now-famous phrase from Pontiac's early print advertisement is still a powerful message for GTO owners.

HANDLING PACKAGE

In addition to the GTO's already firm springs and shocks, an optional handling package could also be specified (code 612). This included stiffer shocks than the standard GTO units and a 20:1 steering gear ratio. The December 1963 issue of *Hot Rod* stated, "The 1964 Tempest is in no way similar to 1963 and earlier Tempests in the handling department. Driving methods used with the GTO would have resulted in 'spinouts' had the test vehicle been a 1963 Tempest." Many automotive enthusiasts have stated similar opinions over the years, confirming that the 1964 models were well-designed purpose-built performance machines.

WHEELS AND TIRES

The 1964 GTO came standard with 14 x 6 steel wheels (compared to 14 x 5 for the Tempest and LeMans) adorned with small hubcaps covering the center of the wheels. These hubcaps, commonly referred to as "poverty caps" or "dog dishes," gave the GTO an unassuming aggressiveness. With certain exterior paint colors, the wheels were color matched to the body when the standard hubcaps were specified; other colors received black-painted wheels.

The look of the 1964 GTO could be drastically altered, depending on which of the optional wheel covers were selected. The Deluxe wheel cover (code 462)

GTOs that were painted Pinehurst Green, Yorktown Blue, Gulfstream Aqua, Singapore Gold, and Saddle Bronze received color-matched wheels when the standard hubcaps were specified. Cars painted Starlight Black also received matching wheels, although the black for the wheels was referred to as Regent Black. This example wears the incorrect 15-inch wheels and tires.

Deluxe wheel covers were an inexpensive option for the 1964 GTO. Unlike the standard "dog-dish" hubcaps, these covered the face of the wheel completely and presented the car with an entirely different appearance.

At $35.50, the Custom wheel covers (sometimes referred to as spinners) were more than double the cost of the Deluxe versions. Beautifully styled, many current GTO owners opt for them, even if their cars were not originally equipped with them.

US Royal Tiger Paw redline tires were standard equipment on the 1964 GTO and contributed greatly to the car's performance aesthetic. With only a 7.5-inch width, these tires were no match for the 428 ft-lbs of torque produced by the 389-ci engine. This GTO wears Coker Tire reproduction redline tires.

featured 10 simulated spokes and covered the entire wheel. This understated version was less aggressive in appearance than the standard hubcaps. The more familiar Custom wheel cover (code 521) displayed eight cooling slots and a spinner center section. Stylish and highly detailed, Custom wheel covers are seen on the vast majority of 1964 GTOs today, even if they were not factory equipped, as many current owners view them as the best-looking of all choices for 1964.

A seldom-seen and, therefore, highly sought after option by collectors are the wire wheel covers. These gave the car a more elegant appearance, in contrast to the more muscular look of other choices.

It's interesting to note that the only available wheel choice for the 1964 GTO was plain 14 x 6 steel wheels. The handsome Rally I wheel did not debut until 1965, followed by the Rally II in 1967.

U.S. Royal Tiger Paw redline tires featuring a 7.5-inch width were standard issue on the 1964 GTO, representing one of the first instances that redline tires were available on an American car. According to Coker Tire, American automobile manufacturers wanted a more aggressive looking tire to better complement the appearance of their new 1964 models and the redline design fit the bill. Whitewall tires were also available on the 1964 GTO at no additional charge, and many GTO buyers opted for them.

However, many current 1964 owners choose redline tires, Tri-Power induction, and a 4-speed manual transmission, even if not factory issued, as this combination seems to represent the epitome of a 1964 Pontiac GTO. For 1965, tire size increased from 7.5 to 7.75 inches, even though the wheels (including the new Rally I) were still sized at 14 x 6 inches.

Today, many GTO owners select modern tires for their classic Pontiacs, preferring the added stability and traction of radials compared to the bias-ply construction of the originals. Companies such as Coker Tire and BFGoodrich now produce redline tires using modern radial technology in sizes that are compatible with original-equipment wheels.

BRAKING SYSTEM

A four-wheel manual braking system, which featured 9.5-inch drums and a single-reservoir master cylinder, was standard equipment for the 1964 GTO (front disc brakes were not available until the 1967 model). The braking components of the 1964 GTO were the same as used on all Tempest and LeMans models, even the base-model 6-cylinder Tempest. Power brakes were an available option for the GTO (code 502) and were denoted by chrome bezels surrounding the accelerator, brake, and clutch pedals (if so equipped).

Considering the high-speed situations that the car and its owner would likely find themselves in, many enthusiasts believed that the brake hardware could have

Chrome trim that surrounds the pedals denotes a car equipped with power brakes. The lack of that trim on this GTO indicates that it is a manual brake car. Visible at the far left next to the brake-release handle is the knob that operates the air vents located in the kick panels.

By studying the interior space of this Saddle Bronze convertible, you can see that this was a well-optioned automobile. A Custom Sports steering wheel, center console, tachometer, push-button radio, and floor mats complement the standard features. Chrome bezels surrounding the brake and accelerator pedals indicate power brakes (code 502).

been further upgraded. In the January 1964 issue of *Motor Trend*, writer Bob McVay noted that the brakes "felt adequate during normal driving, yet heated up and showed considerable fade after half a dozen high-speed stops, but recovered fairly quickly."

Brake fade can occur after repeated or heavy use of the braking system and can ultimately lead to complete brake failure. Although semi-metallic brake shoes were optional hardware and helped to reduce brake fade, they tended to be noisy and many new GTO owners chose the standard brake linings.

Although common during the era, the single-reservoir master cylinder had one major drawback. In the event of a brake fluid leak at any point in the hydraulic system, all fluid could be lost and complete brake failure soon followed. To remedy this problem, a dual-reservoir master cylinder made its debut for the 1967 model year. This feature kept the front and rear braking systems isolated, and allowed at least some braking ability in the event of a fluid leak. The dual-reservoir system was an important safety advancement, and all GTOs from 1967 onward used this arrangement. While front disc brakes appeared as an option for the 1967 model, they did not become standard equipment on the GTO until 1973.

Despite a few shortcomings, the 1964 Pontiac GTO possessed the necessary hardware to be one of the best all-around performance cars of its time. An excerpt from the famed March 1964 issue of *Car and Driver* boasts, "This car does what so many others only talk about. It really does combine brute, blasting performance with balance and stability of a superior nature."

The single-reservoir master cylinder of the 1964 models appears quite diminutive in the large engine compartment, especially when there is no power booster behind it.

Power brakes were available on the 1964 GTO. With this option, the master cylinder was mounted directly to the booster. Upon braking, the power brake option greatly reduced pedal effort for the driver but did not translate into greater braking ability.

The owner of this 1964 GTO converted the car to a dual-reservoir master cylinder. Although not correct for 1964, some owners feel that the added safety benefits are well worth sacrificing originality, particularly for cars that are driven frequently. This car is also equipped with a power brake booster.

Although modern radial tires would noticeably improve handling characteristics, the owner of this Gulfstream Aqua Sports Coupe chose to install reproduction bias-ply redline tires, a concession made to originality.

1964 Pontiac GTO
In Detail No. 8

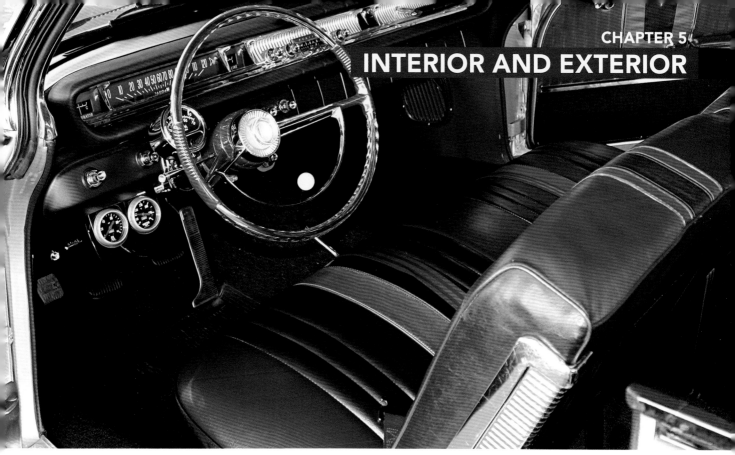

INTERIOR AND EXTERIOR

The attention to detail of the interior in this 1961 Bonneville reflected the fact that it was Pontiac's top model for that year. The interior of this car was restored to factory specifications. A trio of aftermarket gauges was added to monitor the engine's vital signs and are the only deviations from stock.

With the GTO being an option package for the 1964 LeMans, there are many similarities between the two cars, both interior and exterior. Pontiac engineers did, however, include a few details to differentiate the GTO from its lower-performing siblings.

INTERIOR

Inspecting the cabins of Pontiacs from the early 1960s, it's evident that Pontiac Motor Division took great pride in the style and functionality of these spaces. The full-size models, such as the Bonneville and Grand Prix, displayed some of the most beautiful and ornate selections ever offered by an American manufacturer.

Even the sparsely appointed Tempest models were treated to clean, elegant designs that remain attractive well into the 21st Century.

The cabin of the 1964 GTO was nearly identical to that of the 1964 LeMans. Front bucket seats and a rear bench seat were standard on the GTO and available in various colors. The seat pattern was a simple design that incorporated several ribs running from front to back. In addition, a power driver's seat was available at extra cost, although it was quite rare in 1964. Upholstery for the 1965 models was changed to a diagonal pattern that also featured the Pontiac crest within each seat.

The seats and door panels were covered with Morrokide upholstery, a special type of vinyl material that

The interior space of the 1964 GTO is simple, yet tastefully appointed. The influence of Pontiac's full-size cars from the early 1960s is evident. Bucket seats and an engine-turned dash appliqué were standard equipment.

Covered in durable Morrokide vinyl, the 1964 GTO shared the same door panels as the LeMans models and did not display a GTO emblem. The Medium Red upholstery contrasts beautifully with the Cameo Ivory exterior paint.

was durable and wore quite well. Door panels on the 1964 GTO were indistinguishable from those on the 1964 LeMans. This was one of only two years that did not feature a GTO emblem (the 1972 GTO equipped with the LeMans Sport interior was the other). Door panels were redesigned for every model year.

Convertible models received special interior treatment to accommodate the hardware required to operate the top. A narrower rear seat was used, along with uniquely designed rear interior side panels that also featured courtesy lamps. The rear speaker option was not available on the convertible due to limited space and configuration of the top mechanism.

Loop-pile carpeting was color-keyed with the rest of the interior trim, except for cars equipped with parchment interiors; these received black carpet. Color-matched front and rear rubber floor mats were available to protect the carpet from wear and tear. The floor mats could be ordered alone (code 633 for front and rear) or as part of the Protection Group (code 062). This package consisted of floor mats, dash pad, door-edge guards, spare tire cover, rear window defogger, and retractable front seatbelts.

Air conditioning was one of the more expensive options for the 1964 GTO. Known as Tri Comfort air conditioning (code 581), it added $345.60 to the price of the car, $50

Although not commonly seen on the 1964 GTO, power windows were available at extra cost. All four windows could be operated by the switch located on the driver's door.

Rear side panels for convertible models were a distinctive design to accommodate the mechanisms required for top operation. The courtesy lamps were standard on convertibles.

Vinyl floor mats were optional and featured the Pontiac name and crest. These mats included a cutout for the accelerator pedal and displayed the correct contours, which contributed to a proper fit.

Models with factory air conditioning displayed a dashboard that featured vents exclusive to A/C-equipped cars. A/C added 127 pounds to the GTO's weight and $345.60 to the window sticker.

Tastefully adorned with chrome-ribbed trim, the optional center console for the 1964 GTO featured a storage compartment and a courtesy lamp at the rear (shown).

more than the GTO option itself. Due to the added strain on certain components, GTOs equipped with A/C automatically received the heavy-duty radiator and battery. Factory-equipped A/C 1964 GTOs are quite rare, making them highly desirable in today's collector car market.

A center console (code 601) was optional and housed either the automatic or manual shifter (a GTO equipped with the automatic transmission and no console had the shifter mounted on the steering column). Chrome ribs adorned the upper portion of the console, with the lower portion color matched to the other interior components. A hinged lid revealed a storage compartment, and a courtesy lamp was mounted at the rear of the console.

The engine-turned dash appliqué, which surrounded the gauges, was unique to the GTO and provided additional flair. A "GTO" emblem adorned the dash just above the glove box door, notifying passengers that this was no ordinary 1964 Pontiac. A color-keyed two-spoke steering wheel was standard on the GTO and was the same one used on the Tempest and LeMans models; a simulated wood wheel was optional. Known as the Custom Sports steering wheel, it featured a metal four-spoke design with a simulated wood rim.

An excerpt from the March 1964 issue of *Car and Driver* read, "The optional steering wheel is wood-looking plastic that had us completely conned." It went on to state, "Wood or not, it's handsome as hell and an excellent piece of fakery." This four-spoke "wood" steering wheel was exclusive to the 1964 GTO; the optional wheel on the 1965 models was changed to a three-spoke version with a deeper dish.

Instrumentation for the 1964 GTO was adequate but somewhat rudimentary. A 120-mph speedometer, fuel gauge, and simple warning lights pertaining to engine temperature, oil pressure, and battery voltage were standard issue. The problem with such warning lights was that by the time they illuminated to alert the driver, the engine was already experiencing extreme duress. Pulling over and immediately turning off the engine was usually the best option when one of these lights glowed red.

Coolant temperature and oil pressure gauges were not available, but many GTO owners installed aftermarket units to keep a close

The standard two-spoke steering wheel was color keyed to other interior components. This wheel was also used for the 1965 GTO and then changed slightly for the 1966 model, with a completely new design debuting for 1967.

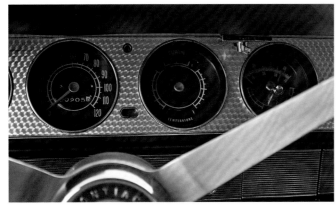

Some enthusiasts opined that the optional in-dash tachometer was difficult to see and somewhat inaccurate. The engine-turned dash appliqué is unique to the 1964 GTO. For 1965, the dash featured a wood-grain pattern, which gave the interior a warmer appearance. The engine-turned appliqué reappeared in 1970–1972, and again in 1974. However, in those instances, the engine-turned portion was much smaller and located beneath the gauges, accenting the larger wood-grain dash surrounds.

The console-mounted vacuum gauge is more for style than performance and was a $29.95 option. Today, it is a prized component among Pontiac collectors.

The optional power antenna was mounted on the passenger-side rear-quarter panel. The switch was located near the center of the dashboard; in this case, near the optional electric clock.

eye on the engine's vital signs. Pontiac understood this need, and a Rally gauge set, including a tachometer as well as oil pressure and coolant temperature gauges, was made available for the 1965 model year.

An in-dash tachometer was an available option for the GTO and complemented the speedometer, occupying the far-right gauge pod. Plagued by visibility and accuracy issues, many owners installed aftermarket units to better monitor the engine RPM. In addition, a console-mounted vacuum gauge could be specified. Although functional, it wasn't the type of instrument demanded by the die-hard enthusiast.

Because of their rarity on early GTO models, power options are now coveted by hobbyists. The standard fixed antenna was fastened to the passenger-side front fender, while the optional power unit was mounted toward the rear section of the passenger-side quarter panel. A switch located near the center of the dash activated the power antenna. This feature was available with both the manual-control and pushbutton radio.

EXTERIOR

The redesigned 1964 Tempest and LeMans models were attractive automobiles, with an authoritative appearance that provided the perfect platform for Pontiac to build its dynamic, new performance car. Fifteen available exterior colors ensured that there was a hue for every GTO buyer.

Twin simulated (non-functional) scoops adorned the GTO's hood, setting it apart from the lesser Tempest and LeMans units, as this hood was not available on those models. Chrome, ribbed inserts gave the GTO a bit of flash that integrated nicely into the overall theme of the car. Some automotive enthusiasts bemoaned the fact that the scoops were nonfunctional and, therefore, simply decorative and unnecessary. Nevertheless, the scoops were an important element in the GTO's design and enhanced its street-tough attitude. The redesigned, center-mounted hood scoop of the 1965 models could be made functional when the Ram Air option was

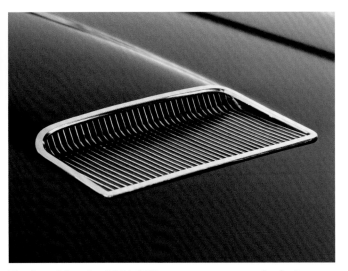

The hood for the 1964 GTO was a one-year-only design and was not used on Tempest or LeMans models. The hood scoops featured stylish chrome-ribbed inserts that accentuated the scoops quite well.

Various GTO callouts were placed strategically throughout the interior and exterior of the car. The elegant fender badges indicated "6.5 Litres," an intentional departure from the common cubic-inch designations.

The Le Mans and GTO grilles received a semi-gloss blackout treatment, but the perimeter and center strips remained chrome plated. A GTO emblem was placed in the driver-side grille.

The grilles for the base Tempest and Tempest Custom display more chrome than those of the Le Mans and GTO models. Fastened to the driver-side grille was a "Pontiac" emblem.

The taillight panel of the 1964 GTO is shared only with the LeMans model. The piece in the center is the fuel filler door; it folds down for access. The 1965 GTO received an updated taillight design, and the fuel filler was relocated behind the license plate.

specified, allowing the engine to take in fresh, cooler air for more horsepower.

Pontiac designers were not shy with the GTO's exterior identification; GTO emblems were placed in the grille, on the quarter panels, and on the deck lid. Stylish badges that boasted "6.5 Litre" were placed on the fenders just behind the wheel opening. Notably, Pontiac was the first American car manufacturer to use "litres" instead of the traditional cubic inches.

The 1964 LeMans and GTO received a different taillight treatment than that of the Tempest and Tempest Custom units. Where the Tempests had taillamps, the LeMans and GTO displayed color-keyed filler panels. The GTO's taillights were somewhat concealed within a ribbed trim panel with red-painted accents. This gave the illusion that the taillights filled the entire rear panel, and a similarity to the 1963 Grand Prix is apparent.

An interesting anomaly for the 1964 models is that the inside trunk area was painted body color, whereas later models used varying shades of gray spatter paint. In addition, an interior trunk release was available and operated by a cable that led to a small pull handle mounted under the dash.

Cordova vinyl tops were available in either ivory or black for the 1964 GTO and presented the car with a slightly more formal aesthetic. Although attractive, vinyl tops were not without their issues. They tended to retain moisture, and this, combined with a propensity by most

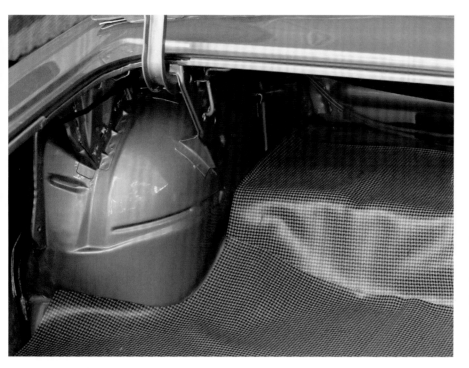

The 1964 models displayed body color inside the trunk space. All models from 1965 onward received varying shades of gray spatter paint. Note the additional body bracing between the wheelwell and the upper portion of the quarter panel on this convertible.

For 1964, the Cordova vinyl top was available in two colors, ivory and black. The Cordova top featured a grain pattern and necessitated some additional trim around its perimeter.

The remote mirror was attached to the upper portion of the driver-side fender and was cable operated. The fixed mirror was mounted in a more traditional location on the driver's door.

manufacturers to use less paint on the roof when a vinyl top was specified, often led to corrosion problems.

Factory two-tone paint was also available for the 1964 GTO and offered in a variety of combinations. The two-tone paint option featured one color on the main part of the body with a contrasting roof color adorned with the same type of trim that accompanied models equipped with a Cordova top. Although not commonly seen, the two-tone 1964 GTOs are quite eye-catching and presented potential buyers yet another way to personalize their new Pontiac.

The convertible tops on the 1964 models were equipped with a soft (plastic) back window, which was used until Pontiac designers changed to glass for the 1968 models. All convertible tops on 1964 GTOs were power operated and offered in six colors: Ivory, Black, Blue, Aqua, Beige, and Saddle.

Driver-side mirrors were optional for the 1964 GTO and two choices were available. The standard mirror was mounted on the door, while the cable-operated remote mirror was affixed to the fender. Research suggests that a passenger-side door mirror was available at the dealer.

In today's automotive world in which numerous safety features are typical, even on entry-level automobiles, it is interesting to discover was and was not available in 1964. Although many 1964 GTOs were well equipped, basic items such as back-up lights were optional features. Front seat belts had to be specifically ordered until January 1964, after which, they became standard equipment but could be deleted if desired (code 414). Considering that a 1964 GTO could be ordered with the 348-hp Tri-Power engine, manual drum brakes, and seat belt delete option, it certainly would have made for a thrilling, if not reckless, driving experience.

Today, when we conjure up images of a 1964 Pontiac GTO, we see redline tires, Tri-Power carburetion, a 4-speed manual transmission, and stylish Custom wheel covers. However, the reality is that most cars were equipped with the 4-barrel carburetor and intake, and many had the 3-speed manual transmission and the basic "dog-dish" hubcaps. It's difficult to fault current 1964 GTO owners, as certain features have become iconic and represent the pinnacle of the GTO legend.

Although most 1964 GTOs displayed them, not all were equipped with a driver-side mirror. This GTO is correctly restored to factory specifications, which did not include passenger- or driver-side mirrors. Although it may have posed a greater challenge for the driver, it certainly presented the car with a clean, uncluttered appearance.

This is a detailed replica of the 1961 Pontiac that David Pearson drove to three NASCAR victories for the Ray Fox racing team that year. The car was sponsored by the Daytona Beach Kennel Club and this re-creation features correct livery and graphics. It is part of a display at The Living Legends of Auto Racing in Daytona, Florida.

Pontiac had been at the forefront of the American racing scene in the late 1950s and early 1960s, earning victories at dragstrips, NASCAR events, and the Bonneville Raceway. Pontiac invested countless resources in honing its high-performance brand, but the GM racing ban of 1963 ceased all factory-backed racing efforts and necessitated Pontiac engineers to develop a new strategy: street performance.

Ironically, it was Pontiac Motor Division's withdrawal from racing that led them to create one of the most iconic production cars of all time: the 1964 GTO. Even without factory support, some competitors continued to successfully campaign Pontiac and Pontiac-powered race cars.

MICKEY THOMPSON

Mickey Thompson's racing accomplishments can, and do, fill entire books, and even though he was not directly involved with the 1964 GTO, his contributions to the Pontiac brand remain unequaled. Thompson was a champion of Pontiac power in the late 1950s and 1960s, and constructed a streamliner race car, *Challenger I*, using four Pontiac V-8 engines backed by heavy-duty Cadillac transmissions.

A streamliner is defined as any machine engineered with an emphasis on aerodynamics, or streamlining, which produces much less resistance compared to traditional designs; it also aids in high-speed stability.

Fireball Roberts is widely recognized for racing full-size Pontiacs with the familiar black and gold paint scheme. He won both the Daytona 500 and the Firecracker 250 races in 1962, piloting a Smokey Yunick–tuned Pontiac. In 1962, Stephens Pontiac in Daytona Beach, Florida, built approximately 30 Fireball Roberts tribute cars to celebrate his success with the Pontiac brand.

The 1964 Pontiac GTO looks great standing still and even better at speed. The 1963 GM racing ban, combined with Pontiac's previous racing experience, resulted in a focus on street performance, and a legend was born.

A man synonymous with speed, Mickey Thompson, poses with one of his most famous machines, *Challenger I*. Powered by four supercharged Pontiac V-8 engines, *Challenger I* achieved a top speed of 406.60 mph at Bonneville International Raceway in September 1960. (Photo Courtesy GM Media Archive)

The Pontiac cross-ram intake manifold was one of many speed parts designed by Mickey Thompson. Curiously, this piece does not display the Thompson name or logo that may have been ground off by a previous owner. Today, items such as this are seldom seen and highly collectible within the Pontiac hobby. In this case, the intake is topped with two Holley 4-barrel carburetors equipped with custom linkage.

Race cars built on this premise could easily be mistaken for rocket ships or heavy artillery, and when combined with the surreal landscape of the Bonneville Salt Flats, they produced sights and sounds experienced nowhere else on the planet.

In the summer of 1959, Mickey Thompson and his *Challenger I* reached an amazing 363.48 mph at Bonneville, a remarkable feat but not enough to break the record of 394.19 mph. Thompson was relentless in his pursuit of speed, and in 1960, he and his team added four 6-71 GMC superchargers to *Challenger I*, one for each of the Pontiac V-8 engines.

On September 9, 1960, Mickey Thompson became the "Fastest Man in the World," driving his streamliner to an astounding 406.60 mph on the Bonneville Salt Flats. A mechanical failure prevented him from executing the required second pass to make the record official, but this event clearly demonstrated the capabilities of Pontiac power and garnered worldwide attention.

In addition to *Challenger I*, Thompson and his crew built other race cars specifically for the Bonneville Salt Flats, including *Attempt I*. This was a smaller car that employed a slingshot-style dragster chassis covered with an aluminum body that somewhat resembled a scaled-down version of *Challenger I*. Power came from a supercharged Pontiac Tempest 4-cylinder engine.

Mickey Thompson was also a successful drag racer, car owner, and in 1955 founder of Lions Drag Strip in Los Angeles, California. Lions was the first track to use the Christmas tree starting system instead of a flagman. A few years later, Jack Chrisman drove Thompson's Pontiac-powered dragster to victory at the 1962 NHRA U.S. Nationals in Indianapolis, Indiana, beating Don Garlits with an 8.76-second elapsed time at 171.75 mph.

Thompson was heavily involved in the performance aftermarket, and working in conjunction with Pontiac, produced some intriguing and now highly sought-after Pontiac engine components.

Pontiac hemi cylinder heads, the result of collaboration between Thompson and Pontiac, are some of the engine parts most prized by Pontiac performance enthusiasts. Featuring a hemispherical combustion chamber, these lightweight aluminum alloy heads allowed for larger valves and ports, and a higher compression ratio, enabling racers to extract the maximum amount of power from their machine.

Thompson also produced blower intake manifolds that allowed racers to install superchargers on their Pontiac engines. A radical, dual 4-barrel cross-ram manifold was another Thompson item, and today it is a collectible piece of Pontiac performance history.

DRAG RACING PERSONALITIES

The Pontiac GTO certainly did not invent competition auto racing, or even street racing. However, it arrived at a moment in history when both the NHRA and NASCAR were gaining in popularity, and public boulevards such as Detroit's Woodward Avenue were the place to be on a Saturday night. Backroads were filled with local gearheads and speed freaks asserting themselves and their machines, vying for automotive superiority.

With Pontiac officially out of racing in 1964 due to the GM racing ban from the previous year, most racing efforts from 1964 onward were private, self-financed campaigns with little or no factory support. From mild to wild, Pontiac performance enthusiasts built fast and viable cars, remaining competitive in all venues.

Scores of Americans were affected by the Vietnam War, and many gearheads were forced to sell or abandon their cars upon being called into military service. This 1964 model proudly wears a Vietnam decal as a reminder of the service and sacrifice made by thousands of American men and women.

71

Racing
Chapter 6

One unique characteristic of the Pontiac V-8 engine is that various displacements appear almost identical, especially the 326- to 455-ci versions. This 462-ci (455 with a .030 overbore) could easily be mistaken for a 389-ci mill. Although the available Tri-Power induction system became closely associated with the GTO, many street and drag racers of the era swapped the factory induction for two 4-barrel carburetors. Combined with an aftermarket aluminum intake manifold, they feed additional air and fuel required in ultra-high-horsepower applications.

Featuring a non-factory color and later Rally II wheels with larger tires, this Pontiac displays subtle hints that it is not a stock restoration and may be packing more power than a factory-issued GTO. It was a lesson that many would-be competitors learned the hard way.

1964 Pontiac GTO
In Detail No. 8

Arnie Beswick

If drag racing ever had a home-town hero, Arnie "The Farmer" Beswick is the one. Hailing from Morrison, Illinois, Beswick boasted a rugged blue-collar background, and epitomized the hardworking American spirit that helped him become a racing legend.

His earliest major drag racing victory was at the first NHRA Nationals in Great Bend, Kansas, in 1955, where he piloted a 1954 Oldsmobile to first place in the B/Stock class. In the wake of mixed results with Dodge in 1956 and 1957, his long-term association with Pontiac was born.

In an interview with Steve Magnante for *Car Craft* magazine, Beswick recalled, "When the Mopars let me down in 1957, I didn't want a Chevy since they were like belly buttons, even then. So I looked at Pontiac and liked the 1957 Tri-Power 347. When it grew to 370 cubes for 1958, I bought one." His 1958 Pontiac performed quite well, but the column-shifter of the 3-speed manual transmission could not withstand repetitive gear slamming, so it was replaced with a BorgWarner T-10 4-speed and a floor-mounted shifter for 1959.

Shortly after purchasing a brand-new 1960 Ventura hardtop from Morrison Pontiac in Clinton, Iowa, Beswick drove it the entire 1,200-mile journey from Illinois to the first NHRA/NASCAR Winternationals

A longtime champion of Pontiacs, Arnie Beswick built this 1964 GTO to compete in the Supercharged/Factory Experimental class. Known as *Mystery Tornado*, the car was virtually brand new with only 16 miles on the odometer when it was transformed into a racer. Here, Beswick and his wife pose for a photo in Daytona Beach, Florida, at a show prior to the 1965 Winternationals. (Photo Courtesy Arnie Beswick)

Powered by a supercharged 421 Super Duty, Arnie Beswick launches *Mystery Tornado* against the Hodges Dodge *Ramcharger*. Beswick states, "Almost every Mopar I had to race against in 1965 had an altered wheelbase." (Photo Courtesy Arnie Beswick)

in Daytona, Florida. His new Ventura came packing the punch of a 389 Tri-Power engine and a floor-shifted 4-speed manual transmission, and had enough muscle to secure the win in the Stock Eliminator class.

When Beswick began making his mark at dragstrips in the southeastern United States, where the payouts were biggest, complaints from local racers resulted in many time-consuming engine tear downs. He recalled, "Pontiac had everything going for it in the early 1960s, and the Chevrolet guys were so damn jealous."

One of Beswick's more noteworthy cars was his famous 1964 Pontiac GTO named *Mystery Tornado*. The GTO began life as a 389 Tri-Power car and Beswick removed the stock engine in favor of a 421 Super Duty, even though the 389 had accrued a mere 16 miles. The 421 powerplant was the same engine used in Beswick's successful *Grocery Getter*, a 1963 Tempest wagon.

A large GMC supercharger was soon added, and *Mystery Tornado* competed in the Supercharged/Factory Experimental class. The car also showcased a lightweight, dealer-installed aluminum front end. Beswick stated, "Pontiac had intentions of selling more of those front ends, but upper management went berserk and stopped it immediately. They sent at least 30 to the crusher and had top-level executives present as witnesses to make sure they got destroyed. That was a direct result of the GM 1963 racing ban; it definitely killed that for us."

With Pontiac (and the rest of General Motors) officially out of racing, the sport was overflowing with Ford and Mopar racers, and dragstrip promoters across the nation wanted a piece of Beswick's one-of-a-kind *Mystery Tornado*. Despite no factory support, Beswick's GTO ran with the best of them, including a long-standing rivalry with Mr. Norm and his Hemi-powered machines and Dyno Don Nicholson in his factory-backed Mercury Comet Cyclone.

Back in Illinois, one of Beswick's neighbors had purchased for his son a brand-new 1964 GTO as a graduation present and Beswick occasionally lent his expertise. He recalled, "I would help him tune it, and it ran great; he wasn't supposed to be racing it, but he was. That car became known as *The Little Farmer* and was even lettered for a little while, until the kid's dad found out and put a stop to it." One can only imagine how wild it must have been to have "The Farmer" in your neighborhood, wrenching on your brand-new GTO.

After nearly two years devoted to racing Pontiacs with no manufacturer help, Beswick decided to accept an offer from Mercury and was soon behind the wheel of a new SOHC 427 Comet Cyclone. The Mercury deal was short-lived, however, as the 427 needed constant adjustments and maintenance. In addition, track promoters and crowds were still clamoring to see Beswick piloting one of his legendary Pontiacs.

Weighing close to 3,500 pounds, *Mystery Tornado* was too heavy to remain competitive against the lightweight Fords and Mopars of the day. Never one to disappoint his fans, Beswick soon focused his attention on morphing his 1963 Super Duty Tempest into

The perennial good neighbor, Arnie Beswick lent his expertise to Phil Reichard and his 1964 GTO, which became known as *The Little Farmer.* When his schedule permitted, Beswick could be spotted behind the wheel of *The Little Farmer* making a quarter-mile pass. (Photo Courtesy Arnie Beswick)

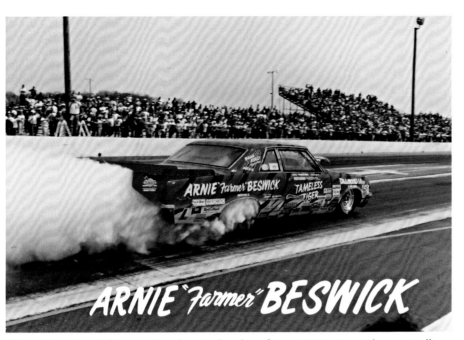

After a long break from racing due to the shop fire in 1972, Beswick eventually built this wild Pro-Mod racer featuring a massive 572-ci engine. Capable of running 7-second quarter-mile times at more than 200 mph, it is one of the fastest cars Beswick has driven. (Photo Courtesy Arnie Beswick)

an altered-wheelbase monster called *Tameless Tiger*. Moving both the front and rear axles forward allowed better weight transfer and increased traction on hard launches. While *Mystery Tornado* was on a full-frame platform, *Tameless Tiger* was unibody construction; this, combined with other weight-saving measures, dropped the heft to approximately 2,800 pounds.

Powered by a supercharged, fuel-injected 421 Super Duty Pontiac, *Tameless Tiger* ran mid-8-second passes in the quarter-mile at nearly 170 mph, and proved to be wildly popular at dragstrips across the nation. Throughout the rest of the 1960s and the first two years of the 1970s, Beswick campaigned numerous Pontiacs in various classes, and in most cases, was highly competitive.

In April 1972, a terrible fire ravaged Beswick's shop, destroying nearly all of his race cars, engines, and tools, along with most of his farm equipment. Arnie slowly but

surely restored his livelihood and returned to racing in 1986, participating in the *Blast from the Past* nostalgia series with a 455-powered 1963 Pontiac Tempest. This somewhat mild race car (by Arnie Beswick standards) fueled his desire to resurrect his own 1963 Tempest, *Tameless Tiger*. With renewed enthusiasm, Beswick was once again burning up the pavement for fans both young and young at heart.

Beswick's continued success led him to develop *Tameless Tiger II*, an outrageous pro-mod race car based on a 1964 GTO. Painted in the familiar orange and black tiger theme, *Tameless Tiger II* featured a fierce 572-ci Pro Stock engine that breathed through a large hood scoop and ripped down the quarter-mile at close to 200 mph.

In August 2003 at a track in Wentzville, Missouri, disaster struck once more, when a nitrous solenoid leaked and caused a massive explosion that consumed Beswick in a fireball. He recalled, "I usually go to these events with another guy to help me out, but he couldn't make it, so I went by myself. I was very busy that day, and someone else had volunteered to help out. I let him work on the car and didn't have time to check everything he did. The bad solenoid blew nitrous under the hood and all down the track. There was an ungodly explosion and I was totally engulfed in flames; the fire was insanely hot." Beswick was severely burned and required a lengthy hospital stay and numerous skin grafts to repair the damage.

Most drivers would have retired from the sport after such a serious accident, but the tough-as-nails Beswick spent the next two years recovering and was racing again by 2005. He explained, "I've always been a low-buck guy, but since the fire, I have to rely on more help. I'm no good at small things, like changing spark plugs, due to all of the skin grafts."

With countless victories spanning more than six decades, Arnie "The Farmer" Beswick is one of the most revered drivers in the history of drag racing. He is the recipient of numerous awards, including 1996 Driver of the Year, and has been inducted to the NHRA Division 3 Hall of Fame. Through tragedy and triumph, Beswick retains his signature small-town charm and appreciation for the sport and the fans that make it all possible.

The Gasser Brothers

Drag cars can take many forms, with some examples resembling their production counterparts, and others reminiscent of rocket ships from an alien planet. A "gas-

ser" somewhat blurs that line. They mostly retain their recognizable factory bodies, but they are heavily modified for the sole purpose of going fast in a straight line. They are a style of drag race car that was popularized in the 1960s and early 1970s. These outrageous machines are defined by their use of a straight axle instead of the stock, independent front suspension. This allows racers to save weight and also provides better weight transfer under hard acceleration. By using a straight axle, the front end becomes much higher than stock and contributes greatly to the menacing appearance of these cars.

Positioning the front of the cars higher off the ground also provides additional clearance for the exhaust, and many racers custom build headers to exit in the front fenderwell area. Large-displacement V-8 engines, often topped with a supercharger for increased

Collectively known as the Gasser Brothers, Dil and Darren Brandow built these two GTOs in the gasser style popularized in the 1960s. Darren's 1965 (left) model features a Don Garlits induction system feeding a 462-ci Pontiac engine. The straight-axle front suspension is clearly visible on both machines and is a defining characteristic of gassers. The 1964 GTO (right) features a 474-ci Pontiac engine topped by a supercharger and two 4-barrel carburetors. (Photo Couresy Dil Brandow)

A large supercharger sits atop the 474-ci Pontiac powerplant and adds a distinctive sound to the car. Gassers often lack conveniences such as air conditioning and power steering, contributing to the stripped-down race-inspired aesthetic. (Photo Courtesy Dil Brandow)

Imposing from all angles, gassers were specifically designed to go fast in a straight line. Here, the custom-built fenderwell headers are shown exiting just behind the front tire. The lack of a hood provides both spectators and competitors with an unobstructed view of the high-horsepower engine. (Photo Courtesy Dil Brandow)

horsepower, are commonplace with gassers. In addition, many are painted with bold metal flake or candy finishes, and these cars are crowd favorites at dragstrips across the country.

Siblings Dil and Darren Brandow (collectively known as the Gasser Brothers) are Pontiac drag race enthusiasts originally from Riverside, California. Together, they have created two of the most wicked Pontiac drag machines to ever rip down the quarter-mile. Dil Brandow remembered, "I was getting bored and started thinking about something different, another brand, maybe a hot rod with a Pontiac engine, but that didn't seem right. I've been a GTO guy all of my life. I thought, 'What if I do something crazy, something *way* outside the box?' So I made a 1/24-scale model of the 1965 *Brutus* GTO and thought, 'How cool would it be to make a real one?' I really wanted a 1965, but a friend in Southern California had a 1964 for sale. That's how it all started."

Dil's GTO, powered by a supercharged 455 Pontiac engine, was bored 0.060 over and displaced 474 ci. It was fitted with Eagle H-beam connecting rods, Ross dished and forged blower pistons, and an Ultra Dyne solid-lifter camshaft. A TH-400 transmission sent the power to a narrowed Ford 9-inch rear end fitted with 3.50 gears and a spool.

Because fenderwell headers are not readily available for Pontiacs, Dil heavily modified a pair originally designed for a small-block Chevrolet, and in conjunction with the Speedway Motors straight-axle kit, they gave his 1964 GTO that signature gasser attitude.

In addition to drag racing, Dil regularly cruised the 1964 GTO on the street, remarking, "Since I built this to be my street hot rod, I didn't have a legal roll bar and was limited to 11.50 and slower in the quarter-mile. So I set up the pulleys to make just enough boost and keep me right there."

After Dil sold his wild 1964 GTO, he began transforming a 1962 Pontiac Tempest into a gasser and preparing his blown 1966 GTO race car for the strip.

ROAD RACE COMPETITORS

When most muscle car and GTO enthusiasts think about racing, they usually conjure up images of their local dragstrip or late-night street racing in short, 1/8-mile bursts on the outskirts of their hometown. The stinging scent of burnt rubber and high-octane race fuel is an intoxicating mixture to some, but there is a whole other side to motorsports that many muscle car fans know little about: road racing.

Gray Ghost

The 1964 Pontiac known as *Gray Ghost* is likely the most recognized road race GTO. Campaigned in the 1971 Trans-Am series by then–Pontiac senior engineer Herb Adams, along with fellow engineers Tom Nell and Joe Brady, *Gray Ghost* is yet another great underdog story and an inspiring example of what can be done with the venerable Pontiac V-8 engine and some ingenuity.

Herb Adams started at Pontiac in 1957, attending the General Motors Institute, which was a co-op program that provided young students with real-world experience. It was becoming a very exciting time to be at Pontiac Motor Division and Herb Adams reflected, "DeLorean was great; Knudsen, Estes, and DeLorean really cranked up Pontiac, and got it making money."

Herb Adams became part of a group of engineers who supplied engines to the Jerry Titus team for the upcoming season, and it proved to be quite a challenge. Adams remembered, "In 1969, John DeLorean decided to support the Titus-Godsall racing team with engine development. The Chrysler and Ford engines were making 450 to 470 hp, but our first Pontiac race engine was only putting out around 300." We were two years behind those other teams. The one good thing that came from that was we figured out what would work. We eventually knew how to build a good Pontiac."

Adams, Nell, and Jeff Young worked diligently to improve the power output from their

The 1964 Pontiac LeMans turned GTO known as *Gray Ghost* is another true underdog story. Pontiac Engineer Herb Adams and his crew campaigned this machine in the 1971 Trans-Am racing series. The car belonged to Adams' wife before she consented to letting him convert it into what became one of the most well known road race Pontiacs in history. (Photo Courtesy Ted Lambiris)

At the behest of John DeLorean, Herb Adams and other engineers began supplying engines for the Titus-Godsall racing team. Despite initial difficulty in achieving ample power, the team persisted and became fluent in building small-displacement Pontiac engines for maximum horsepower.

Gray Ghost chases down an early Mustang at a nostalgia event. *Gray Ghost* has recently been restored and will compete at upcoming Historic Trans-Am Series events. (Photo Courtesy Don Keefe)

small-displacement Pontiac mill, eventually producing an impressive 475 hp.

Gray Ghost began as a 1964 Pontiac LeMans that belonged to Herb Adams' wife and was used as her daily mode of transportation. The car was in decent shape but a long way from being a competitive race car. After a promise from Herb that she would receive a new car, Mrs. Adams gave her husband permission to transform her 1964 Pontiac into a Trans-Am series racer.

An early incarnation of *Gray Ghost* featured a Pontiac 326 engine and a Powerglide 2-speed automatic transmission. Adams and his crew, which became the Trans-Action race team, were just beginning to get a feel for the car. Herb Adams himself piloted *Gray Ghost* on local road courses during these early test runs.

With no factory support from Pontiac, but with increasing confidence in the car and themselves, the "Trans-Action" team decided to self-finance their 1971 Trans-Am series effort, competing against bigger teams with much deeper pockets. "We didn't have the money for a new Camaro; we just wanted to show those other guys what we could do," said Adams.

Using a de-stroked Pontiac 400 engine to stay below the 5.0-liter maximum engine size per Trans-Am series rules, Adams and crew applied knowledge gleaned from the Titus-Godsall effort, generating an impressive 470 hp from just 303 ci. Adams recalled, "Jeff Young built a flow bench, and we worked hard on cylinder head flow, the design of the ports, and the cam timing, eventually getting to about 470 hp with a 7,500-rpm shift point."

The Trans-Am series was created in 1966 by John Bishop, president of the Sports Car Club of America (SCCA). The series played host to some of the biggest names and best cars of the era, including Mark Donohue and the Chevrolet Camaro (later the AMC Javelin), Sam Posey and the Dodge Challenger, and Jerry Titus, who had achieved success driving a Ford GT350 for the Carroll Shelby team. Titus made the switch to Pontiac late in 1968 when he partnered with Terry Godsall as co-owner of the Titus-Godsall race team before his untimely death in August 1970 from injuries sustained in a crash at Road America in Elkhart Lake, Wisconsin.

Divided into two classes: Under 2.0 Liter and Over 2.0 Liter, the first Trans-Am series race was held at Sebring International Raceway in Sebring, Florida, in 1966. The Under 2.0 Liter class showcased brands such as Porsche, Datsun, and Alfa Romeo; the Over 2.0 Liter class (which was limited to 5.0 liters) featured the heftier V-8–powered American muscle cars.

Legendary racer Mark Donohue's Trans-Am career began in 1967, when he won three races driving the now-famous blue Chevrolet Camaro for the Roger Penske

Three 1970 Pontiac Trans-Ams were built for the Titus-Godsall race team. Tragically, Jerry Titus died in August of 1970 from a crash at Road America in Elkhart Lake, Wisconsin. This car, one of the remaining original Titus-Godsall 1970 Pontiacs, is now owned and driven by Rob Kauffman and regularly competes in the Historic Trans-Am Series.

Mark Donohue drove the number-15 Chevrolet Camaro during the 1967 Trans-Am season. A highly competitive car, it featured an acid-dipped body to reduce weight and increase handling. Rival drivers became suspicious at the final race of the season in Seattle, Washington, when the Camaro was much faster than any other car in the field. Although a post-race measurement found the car to be 250 pounds underweight, the victory was allowed to stand.

Mark Donohue was already an accomplished race car driver by the time he began competing in the Trans-Am series. In 1971, he was nearly unstoppable, winning seven races in the Penske Racing AMC Javelin.

race team. Donohue scored 10 wins in 1968 and 6 in 1969, quickly making a name for himself in the series.

In 1970, the Penske race team campaigned AMC Javelins. These cars eventually became synonymous with Mark Donohue, and he won three Trans-Am races that year.

Competition in the Trans-Am series was fierce, and the 1971 season in which *Gray Ghost* vied was no exception. Herb Adams and crew selected Bob Tullius, who had piloted a Dodge Dart to victory in the inaugural Over 2.0 Liter class in 1966, to drive *Gray Ghost* for their 1971 race effort against Donohue and other skilled drivers such as George Follmer and Peter Revson. However, Donohue was nearly unbeatable, winning an amazing 7 out of 10 races behind the wheel

of the number-6 Penske AMC Javelin, solidifying his reputation as an elite Trans-Am racer. AMCs proved to be formidable opponents that year, finishing first, second, and third at the Riverside International Raceway event in Riverside, California.

Mark Donohue is still considered one of the most accomplished race car drivers of all time. In addition to his Trans-Am series mastery, career highlights include a fourth-place finish at the 24 Hours of Le Mans in 1967 and winning the Indianapolis 500 in 1972. Donohue also worked closely with Porsche in 1971 and 1972, testing and refining the 917/10 and, later, 917/30 models. With the 917/30, he set a top-speed record at Talladega Superspeedway in 1975 with an average speed of 221.12 mph.

and was a crowd pleaser at every event. The Trans-Action team returned to the Trans-Am series in 1972 with a Firebird Formula known as *Junkyard Firebird,* driven by Milt Minter, thinking that it would be more competitive than *Gray Ghost.*

Herb Adams applied much of what he learned with the 303 engine in the Trans-Am series to what eventually became the 455 Super Duty. Adams remembered, "The very first 455s we built were high compression and close to 600 hp. To meet federal law, the compression was lowered to 8.4:1 and the engine was drastically detuned. After I left Pontiac, other engineers took over the project and detuned it even more."

Adams parted ways with Pontiac Motor Division in 1973,

Herb Adams was instrumental in the development of many high-performance programs at Pontiac, including the Trans Am and 455 Super Duty engine. Here, he poses next to one of his later achievements a Pontiac Fire Am, which improved upon the already exciting Trans Am model. (Photo Courtesy Herb Adams)

Seasoned racer Bob Tullius was behind the wheel of *Gray Ghost* for the Trans-Action team, including the first race on the 1971 Trans-Am series calendar at Lime Rock Park in Connecticut. Heavy rains soaked the track and the drivers had little control of their finely tuned race cars, except Tullius and *Gray Ghost.*

The "old" 1964 Pontiac handled much better in the poor conditions than most of the competition, and Herb Adams recalled, "Tullius was just damn good in the rain, and the bigger tires up front really helped." Tullius had worked his way up from the back of the pack to second place, when a head gasket failed and took him out of the race. While it was disheartening for the crew, it showed the competition that the Pontiac could keep pace with the smaller and newer Javelins, Camaros, and Mustangs.

Gray Ghost entered just six races in the 1971 season but completed the year with three top-five finishes

where he was still considered "one of DeLorean's guys," a label not viewed favorably by Pontiac's new management. Adams then founded Very Special Equipment (VSE), which created the Fire Am performance package. The Fire Am package could take a stock Firebird or Trans Am and transform it into a well-balanced performance machine.

A handful of Fire Ams were sold at Pontiac dealerships, but the majority of the cars were built from mail-order components offered in stages, from Stage 1, which consisted of minor suspension upgrades, to road race–ready Stage 3 offerings that featured major suspension, braking, and driveline enhancements.

Herb Adams' expertise and ingenuity was influential in producing some of the most renowned Pontiacs in the history of the brand, and today he is considered a legend in the automotive community.

Stellhorn originally used a Pontiac 455-ci engine de-stroked to 440 ci in his GTO, but reliability issues forced him to switch to LS3 power. The LS3 makes more than 600 hp and can withstand the continuous high-RPM use that is typically seen in a road race car. (Photo Courtesy Don Stellhorn)

Don Stellhorn

A diehard Pontiac enthusiast, Don Stellhorn owns one of the most uncompromising 1964 GTOs on the planet. Custom engineered from the ground up, its combination of handling, power, and braking ability is unparalleled. "I wanted to create a "what if" scenario, if those Trans-Am teams from the late 1960s and early 1970s had no rules," he said.

Stellhorn started with a bare 1964 Pontiac GTO frame, and then custom-built a three-link rear suspension featuring Aldan Eagle adjustable shocks, Hyperco springs, and a stout .875-inch sway bar.

The front suspension modifications began with Stellhorn boxing in the frame and fabricating new mounting points for the control arms. He then custom-made the center link and shortened the steering arms to clear the massive wheel and tire combination. A large 1.5-inch sway bar from Schroeder Racing completed the front-end treatment.

The braking system on a road racer endures much more abuse than the brake components of a street car or even a drag car. Races cover many miles and brakes take a tremendous amount of punishment. Stellhorn's Pontiac employs Wilwood GT-III calipers and 13-inch Coleman rotors up front and Wilwood Forged Billet Superlite calipers with 12-inch Coleman rotors out back. Huge CCW 17 x 12.5 wheels hold the Kuhmo 335/35/17 race radials.

Stellhorn's machine was originally raced using traditional Pontiac power. Starting with a 455 block, it was bored 0.035 over and fitted with a 428 crankshaft, resulting in 440 ci. In a 2008 article by Christopher R. Phillip for *High Performance Pontiac*, Stellhorn explained, "Since it has a shorter stroke of 4.00 inches, the motor revs quicker than a 455 ever could, and with higher RPM potential, it loves to pull to 6,500 and wants more. Outfitted with a 2.75:1 gear ratio, the GTO will do 180 mph at 6,700 rpm."

Stellhorn extracted a substantial amount of power from the Pontiac 440, peaking at about 585 hp, but consistently high engine-oil temperatures forced him to switch to an LS3 powerplant in 2011. Stellhorn said, "With the LS3 engine, I can run all day long and any parts I need are available quickly. With the 440 Pontiac, it only lasted about three laps before the oil temperature was 300 degrees and climbing."

Shifting is done manually, with a Muncie M-22 transmission featuring a heavy-duty case and a Spec Stage 2 clutch. An aluminum driveshaft connects the gearbox to the Ford 9-inch rear end, which uses 1.0-degree negative-camber NASCAR hubs.

Competing at tracks such as Pocono Raceway, Watkins Glen, and Virginia International Raceway, Don Stellhorn and his 1964 GTO represent one man's life-long affinity for Pontiac and the desire to improve upon a legendary machine.

Whether for the street, strip, or road course, loyal enthusiasts continue to build high-performance Pontiacs for competition use, drawing inspiration from automotive legends. The 1964 Pontiac GTO, its predecessors, and its successors have left an indelible mark on the world of automotive competition.

Don Stellhorn's 1964 GTO is an impressive combination of classic and modern styling. The road racer features many custom-built chassis, suspension, and braking components, making it one of the best corner-carving GTOs in the world. (Photo Courtesy Don Stellhorn)

CHAPTER 7

END OF AN ERA

To this day, many automotive enthusiasts consider the 1964 Pontiac GTO to be the first muscle car. Although the GTO had some ups and downs throughout its lifespan, it has made history as a true American classic and earned its place in the pantheon of automotive icons.

Performers often speak about "ending on a high note," leaving the audience wanting more, and thus, enhancing their status. For some, overstaying one's welcome is tantamount to complete failure, and in many cases, that proves to be true. Consider the beloved Pontiac GTO, riding a wave of immense popularity and cultural significance from its debut in 1964 to the peak of the muscle car era in 1970. With its roaring engine, muscular profile, and youthful appeal, teenagers dreamed of owning one, and songs were written about them. The Judge models were even named after a skit from the hip television show, *Rowan and Martin's Laugh-In,* which aired from 1968 to 1973.

However, like many things, the GTO ran its course. Beginning in 1971, the GTO was already lacking some of the power and allure that made people fall in love with it in the first place. Although these models still retained some of the original glory from previous years with their stylish bodies, bold colors, and large V-8 engines, reduced compression ratios and stricter emissions standards began to have a negative effect on performance.

Air quality concerns and the gas crisis in 1973 altered the priorities of the American car-buying public, and by this time, the performance decline was obvious. Compression for the 400-ci engine was an anemic 8.0:1 and sales dropped to a paltry 4,806 units. Plans for a

455 Super Duty 1973 GTO never came to fruition, as Pontiac seemed to be focusing its efforts on the Firebird/ Trans Am lineup and the new Grand Am. The division even went as far as offering the stylish urethane nose piece on the Grand Am, not the GTO, which received an uninspired header panel and bulky chrome bumper.

Things changed drastically again in 1974, with the GTO now based on the Chevrolet Nova (X-Body). The

Some Pontiac enthusiasts consider the 1970 model to be the embodiment of a GTO. Aggressive styling, bold colors, and the availability of high-horsepower engines such as the Ram Air IV 400 and the torque monster 455 H.O. appealed to a vast array of potential buyers. This modified Cardinal Red 1970 Judge wears larger aftermarket wheels and tires. The exhaust is routed to exit just behind the rear wheels, similar to the 1972 models. (Photo Courtesy Chris Phillip)

Although it is a handsome car and presents extremely well, many Pontiac purists dismissed the 1973 GTO when it first debuted. The styling was shared (for the most part) with the Grand Am and LeMans models and was a radical departure from the chiseled look of the 1970–1972 GTOs. With production at just 4,806, the 1973 GTO is now a rare and collectible piece of Pontiac history. (Photo Courtesy Chris Phillip)

Although the similarity to the Chevrolet Nova is apparent, Pontiac included some of its signature styling cues in the design of the 1974 GTO. The split grille, functional shaker hood scoop, and familiar Rally II wheels helped to separate the car from its corporate cousins. While sales improved to 7,058 units, the 1974 GTO was not considered a success and was the last GTO produced until the 2004 model. (Photo Courtesy Chris Phillip)

only available engine was a timid 350-ci mill with 7.6:1 compression rated at just 200 hp. The relatively small engine was intended as a way to keep insurance premiums affordable while attaining better gas mileage. Although the 1973 and 1974 GTOs paled in comparison to their older siblings, it's worth noting that Pontiac's offerings were still more potent than those of most other American manufacturers. Compared to a car such as the 1974 Ford Mustang II, the later GTOs suddenly seem adequate, even impressive.

In retrospect, with a few bold moves by Pontiac management and a different political climate, the GTO could have indeed ended on a high note. Imagine the possibilities if the compact and lightweight 1974 GTO were treated to a 455 Super Duty option. While perhaps not generating huge sales, it certainly would have been a fitting end to the storied legend of the Pontiac GTO and would stand tall beside the renowned 1964 model

that won over the hearts and minds of a generation just 10 years prior.

REBIRTH

Using the Australian Holden Monaro platform, General Motors created a fourth-generation GTO from 2004 to 2006. Despite the fact that it was equipped with a 5.7-liter 350-hp LS1 engine and an available 6-speed manual transmission, the reception by the automotive community was underwhelming. The most common critique of the Aussie GTOs was that the styling was too conservative and bland, lacking the assertive visual impact of its predecessors. In the December 2003 issue of *Car and Driver*, Aaron Robinson wrote, "The new GTO's styling is a snooze." Robinson went on to praise nearly every other aspect of the car, but his initial statement echoed what most other performance car enthusiasts were saying.

In an interview with Jeff Koch for *Hemmings Classic Car*, Jim Wangers recalled, "It takes 24 months for the government to certify a car for emissions and aerodynamics to assess gas mileage estimates. The GTO came to market in 18 months, really. They tried to get a hood scoop by, but the government grumped that it altered airflow over the car. Somehow, the Pontiac guys convinced the government that the GTO with a flat hood was enough like the new 2004 Grand Prix that they let it piggyback onto the Grand Prix's federalization."

Many of the concerns about the 2004 GTO were addressed with the 2005 model; scoops were added to the otherwise lifeless hood and the dual exhaust exited out the back on either side of the rear bumper, resulting in a more classic muscle car appearance. A 6.0-liter LS2

To most enthusiasts, the 2005 and 2006 GTOs were a huge improvement over the 2004 models. The addition of hood scoops and a dual-exit exhaust presented the car with a more aggressive appearance. This beautiful Phantom Black 2006 GTO recaptures the youthful spirit and possesses the raw power that made the original GTO the legend that it is today.

The 2008–2009 G8s were Pontiac's last true high-performance car. This 2008 G8 GT features a 6.0-liter 361-hp engine and a modern suspension that is ideal for corner carving. The owner of this G8 added aftermarket wheels and tires, along with larger brakes from a Cadillac CTS-V.

engine with 400 hp replaced the previous year's 5.7-liter powerplant and lasted through the 2006 production. The 2005 and 2006 models were nearly identical, with only small interior refinements and a few new color choices differentiating the two.

Even though the Australian-built GTOs outperform their ancestors from the 1960s and 1970s in nearly every category, many Pontiac enthusiasts did not consider the 2004–2006 Australian-built models to be "real" GTOs, creating a strong division within the hobby. One can speculate that the 2004–2006 examples may have been more successful if they had not carried the GTO badge; they would not have drawn constant comparisons to the cherished vintage models.

Sales figures for the three model years of 2004–2006 were well below GM's initial estimates of 18,000 to 20,000 per year, with total production just under 40,800 (sources cite varying production figures for the 2004 model). The poor sales were reminiscent of the much-maligned 1973 and 1974 GTOs, with 4,806 and 7,058 units, respectively, which caused the Australian versions to be unfairly classified with the lower-performing GTOs.

In 2008, Pontiac again looked to the Australia for a performance automobile to bring to the U.S. market. The Pontiac G8 was a four-door sedan based on the Holden Commodore and was produced from 2008 to 2009. With an aggressive appearance, it did not share the criticism experienced by the 2004–2006 GTOs.

The base G8 was equipped with a 3.6-liter V-6, producing 256 hp. A GT model with a 6.0-liter V-8 churning out 361 hp and 385 ft-lbs of torque was also available. In 2009, a GXP model was offered, possessing a slightly detuned 6.2-liter V-8 borrowed from the Corvette; it pumped out an impressive 402 hp and 402 ft-lbs of torque.

Even though the G8 was a four-door sedan, most aficionados agree that Pontiac "got it right." The combination of an authoritative, well-designed exterior and a powerful engine stayed true to Pontiac's performance persona.

VALUE AND COLLECTIBILITY

Pontiac GTOs of all years are coveted by automotive collectors, and because the 1964 model was the first year of production, it's even more desirable. Ironically, the lower-performing 1973 and 1974 GTOs are also highly desirable, due to their low production numbers. As with all collector cars, condition, originality, and optional equipment play a huge role in determining value.

A rotisserie-restored 1964 GTO convertible sold for $82,500 at the 2013 Barrett Jackson auction in Scottsdale, Arizona. Painstakingly detailed, it was a beautiful example of the beloved 1964 model. In contrast, a 1964 GTO two-door hardtop sold for $29,700 at the 2015 Barrett Jackson event in Palm Beach, Florida. The latter car featured a Tri-Power and 4-speed transmission that was not original to the car, along with cylinder heads from a later engine, which obviously contributed to the much lower price.

A quick search of a popular online auction site revealed a driver-quality 1964 convertible offered at just under $33,000. This car displayed a non-original Tri-Power system and a 4-speed manual transmission instead of the factory-issued 2-speed automatic. Although not completely original and needing some minor engine and interior detailing, the price appeared to be appropriate for today's collector car market.

An online classified ad revealed a meticulously detailed 1964 GTO hardtop offered at $67,400. A frame-off restoration, it has won "Best of Show" at the Pontiac Nationals and "First Prize" at the 2015 Antique Automobile Club of America show. Originally equipped with a 4-barrel, it now features Tri-Power induction, the only deviation from stock. The 4-speed manual transmission and Safe-T-Track rear end are said to be original and refurbished to factory specifications. Finished in Aquamarine with Dark Aqua upholstery, this Pontiac certainly appears to be a wonderful example of a first-year GTO.

With only 6,644 GTO convertibles produced in 1964, they are highly sought after by automotive collectors. This Yorktown Blue model features a black interior with a matching black top, Tri-Power induction, power windows, and Custom wheel covers. A 1964 GTO convertible with power windows is quite rare, therefore increasing its collectability.

LEGACY

More than five decades after the first Pontiac GTO was created, we are in yet another automotive renaissance period; the long-standing rivalries between General Motors, Ford, and Chrysler have a renewed vigor, and manufacturers are offering more powerful combinations than ever before. The current versions of the Chevrolet Camaro, Ford Mustang, and Dodge Challenger are well designed, paying tribute to the iconic muscle cars of the 1960s and 1970s, while featuring an outstanding combination of horsepower and fuel economy.

It's a bit ironic that both the car and manufacturer that ignited an automotive revolution no longer exist; the last Pontiacs were sold in 2010. Jim Wangers offered some insight as to why General Motors made the decision to drop Pontiac. "Well, Buick was a huge success in the Chinese market; it was a stroke of genius, really. GM took a car that was basically a Chevy, stuck some portholes on the fenders, and they loved it. It was kind of a bastard, but in a good way. Even though Pontiac outsold Buick four to one in the U.S., Pontiac was never really a popular export car. GM didn't want to compromise the success with Buick in China, so they dropped Pontiac."

Political factors were also at play, and General Motors was required to eliminate four of its brands to receive federal aid as part of its bankruptcy agreement. Pontiac, Saturn, Saab, and Hummer were discontinued.

Despite the fact that Pontiac has not produced a car in more than six years, there are legions of devoted fans worldwide, and the hobby is thriving. Publications such as *Poncho Perfection* and *Smoke Signals* are great resources for any Pontiac lover, showcasing the brand's history, technical articles, and full features on some of the nicest Pontiacs in the world. Scores of restoration and high-performance parts are now readily available to the Pontiac aficionado, and the desire for new Pontiac automobiles is strong, with several efforts trying to persuade General Motors to revive the brand.

After a hiatus from 2003 to 2009, Chevrolet brought back the popular Camaro and, along with the Ford Mustang and Dodge Challenger, reinvigorated the muscle car hobby. The fifth- and sixth-generation Camaros feature styling traits from the first-generation cars blended with an edgy, contemporary form. These models are also the platform upon which companies such as Trans Am Depot produce their exciting, new Trans Am– and GTO–inspired performance cars.

Located in Tallahassee, Florida, Trans Am Depot converts fifth-generation Camaros into modern Trans Am and GTO models. This version, known as a "6T9," is derived from the popular 1969 GTO Judge and features fully functioning hideaway headlights. These machines can be custom ordered with engine options starting at 550 hp all the way to 840 hp, ensuring that there is ample performance to back up its street-tough appearance. (Photo Courtesy Trans Am Depot)

Bringbackpontiac.org and several other social media initiatives are at the forefront of this movement. However, global economics and factory retooling, among other hurdles, make it unlikely that General Motors will ever bring back Pontiac Motor Division.

To satiate the hunger of many Pontiac devotees, companies such as Trans Am Depot of Tallahassee, Florida, have filled a void by creating stunning new Trans Am and GTO models, using the fifth-generation Chevrolet Camaro as a platform. Custom-built front and rear fascias, hoods, taillights, and wheels are just a few of the items installed to make this transformation. Using state-of-the-art technology, T-tops similar to the ones from iconic Trans Am models from the late 1970s and early 1980s can be fitted to these cars. Trans Am Depot's world-class facility and skilled craftsmen ensure that these cars are of the highest caliber and are a welcome addition to the Pontiac hobby.

Today, the 1964 Pontiac GTO is still widely considered to be the first muscle car and has rightfully earned its place in automotive and American history. It kick-started a phenomenon and changed people's expectations of what an American car could be. It was much more than a just a performance car, it was an *attitude*. Muscle car enthusiasts should be ever grateful for that meeting between John DeLorean, Bill Collins, and Russ Gee at the GM Proving Grounds in early 1963. Collins' off-the-cuff remark led to the creation of one of the most memorable cars in the world: "You know, John, it would take us about a half hour to stick a 389 in this thing."

Cars such as this beautiful Starlight Black hardtop with black interior and black vinyl top are often referred to as "triple black" cars. This particular car is a 348-hp Tri-Power with 4-speed manual transmission, no side mirrors, and seat belt delete, making for an exhilarating and daring driving experience.

PRODUCTION FIGURES

1964 PONTIAC GTO PRODUCTION FIGURES

Body	Model Number	Production
Hardtop	2237	18,422
Sports Coupe	2227	7,384
Convertible	2267	6,644
Total Production		32,450

PRODUCTION BY ENGINE TYPE

Engine	HP	Production
389 4-barrel	325	24,205
389 Tri-Power	348	8,245
Total Production		32,450

Note: Transmission production figures are not available for the 1964 GTO.

INTERIOR, EXTERIOR AND CORDOVA/CONVERTIBLE TOP COLORS

1964 PONTIAC GTO PAINT CODES

Paint Code	Color
A	Starlight Black
C	Cameo Ivory
D	Silvermist Gray
F	Yorktown Blue
H	Skyline Blue
J	Pinehurst Green
L	Marimba Red

Paint Code	Color
N	Sunfire Red
P	Aquamarine
Q	Gulfstream Aqua
R	Alamo Beige
S	Saddle Bronze
T	Singapore Gold
V	Grenadier Red
W	Nocturne Blue

1964 PONTIAC GTO CORDOVA AND CONVERTIBLE TOP CODES

Code	Color
1	Ivory
2	Black
4	Blue
5	Aqua
6	Beige
7	Saddle

Note: Cordova tops only available in Ivory and Black.

INTERIOR COLOR CODES

Code*	Color
214	Black
215	Dark Blue
216	Light Saddle
217	Dark Aqua
218	Medium Red
219	Parchment

* with bucket seats

1964 PONTIAC LEMANS OPTIONS LIST

Sales Code	UPC Code	Description	SRP
2227		LeMans Sports Coupe	$2,480.00
2237		LeMans Hardtop Coupe	2,545.00
2267		LeMans Convertible	2,785.00
061		Basic Group with W62 GTO option: includes 392, 421, 471 (for manual transmission cars)	92.59
061		Basic Group with W62 GTO option: includes 392, 421, 471 (for automatic transmission cars)	90.44
062		Protection Group: includes 424, 512, 541, 572, 624, 633 (Sports Coupe and Hardtop)	64.66
062		Protection Group: includes 424, 512, 572, 624, 633 (Convertible)	43.14
081		Mirror Group: includes 441, 442, 444	17.48
084		Lamp Group: includes 404, 481, 482, 484, 491, 492, 494 (Sports Coupe and Hardtop)	30.71
084		Lamp Group: includes 404, 481, 482, 491, 492, 494 (Convertible)	18.02
382	W62	GTO Group (LeMans Sports Coupe, Hardtop, and Convertible only)	295.90
392	U63	Radio: Push Button with Manual Antenna (some PMD literature prices this option at $88.77 for Convertible)	62.41
393	U63	Radio: Push Button with Electric Antenna (some PMD literature prices this option at $118.52 for Convertible)	92.16
398	U60	Radio: Manual Control with Manual Antenna	53.80
399	U60	Radio: Manual Control with Electric Antenna	83.55
401	U80	Rear Speaker, Sepra-Phonic (not available with Convertible)	14.15
402	C13	Wipers, Dual-Speed Electric	4.84
404	U26	Lamp, Underhood	3.55
411	A20	Front Seat Belts (prior to January 1964)	10.76
411	N95	Wheel Discs, Wire	69.40
412	B50	Cushion, Custom Foam Front (not applicable for bucket seats)	8.07
414	A48	Seat Belt Delete, credit (after December 1963)	-11.00
421	C11	Dual-Speed Wipers with Washer	17.27
422	N25	Extensions, Tailpipe	21.30
424	B70	Pad, Instrument Panel	16.14
431	K45	Air Cleaner, Heavy-Duty (standard with GTO package)	4.84
432	V01	Radiator, Heavy-Duty (included with air conditioning)	15.06
434	C06	Power Top (standard with GTO package)	53.80
441	D34	Mirror, Visor Vanity	1.45
442	D31	Mirror, Inside Non-Glare	4.25
444	D33	Mirror, Outside LH Remote	11.78
451	Y91	Deck Lid, Remote	11.78
452	U16	Tachometer	53.80
454	N33	Steering Wheel, Tilt (requires power steering)	43.04
462	P01	Wheel Discs, Deluxe	15.60
471	T86	Lamps, Back-up (manual transmission)	12.91
471	T86	Lamps, Back-up (automatic transmission)	10.76
474	U84	Rear Speaker, Verbra-Phonic (not available with Convertible)	53.80
481	U25	Lamp, Luggage	3.55
482	U27	Lamp, Glove Box	2.85
484	C86	Lamp, Dome and Reading (not available with Convertible)	8.39

Sales Code	UPC Code	Description	SRP
491	U29	Lamp, Courtesy (standard with Convertible)	$4.30
492	U28	Lamp, Ashtray and Lighter	3.12
494	U40	Lamp, Parking Brake	4.95
501	N40	Power Steering	96.84
502	J50	Power Brakes	42.50
511	N10	Exhaust, Dual (standard with GTO package)	30.88
512	B93	Door Edge Guards	4.84
521	P02	Wheel Discs, Custom	35.50
524	N34	Steering Wheel, Custom Sports	39.27
531	A01	Glass, Soft Ray, All Windows	31.20
532	A02	Glass, Soft Ray, Windshield	19.91
541	C50	Defogger, Rear Window (not available with Convertible)	21.52
551	A31	Power Windows	102.22
564	A46	Power Driver's Seat	71.02
572	P17	Cover, Spare Tire	2.58
581	C60	Air Conditioner, Tri-Comfort	345.60
582	T60	Battery, Heavy-Duty (standard with air conditioning)	3.55
584	C48	Heater Delete (credit)	-73.00
592		Special Request Items	varies
601	D55	Center Console	48.15
602	D32	Mirror, Outside Rearview	4.25
604	U35	Electric Clock	19.37
612	Y96	Rally Handling Kit	16.14
614	K24	Positive Crankcase Ventilation (available after December 1963)	5.38
621	F40	Heavy-Duty Springs and Shocks (cars with W62 GTO option automatically received H-D Springs)	3.82
622	G66	Superlift Rear Shocks	40.35
624	A49	Seatbelts, Front Pair	18.29
631	B32	Floor Mats, Front	6.24
632	B33	Floor Mats, Rear	5.81
644	K08	Fan, Heavy-Duty	3.12
671	K66	Transistor Ignition	75.27
692	J65	Metallic Brake Linings	36.86
701	G81	Safe-T-Track Differential	37.66
702		Standard Axle	No Charge
809	L71	389 Tri-Power Engine (GTO only)	115.78
77W	M20	4-Speed Synchromesh Transmission, Wide-Ratio (except 3.90 axle)	188.30
779	M20	4-Speed Synchromesh Transmission, Wide-Ratio (3.90 axle)	188.30
778	M21	4-Speed Synchromesh Transmission, Close-Ratio, available after March 1964 (requires GTO package, Tri-Power, 3.90 axle, metallic brake linings, Safe-T-Track rear end, heavy-duty fan, and heavy-duty radiator)	175.00
77J	M31	2-Speed Automatic Transmission	199.06
RTT		Two-Tone Paint (not available on Convertible)	31.74
SPS		Single Color, Special Paint	40.19
SVT		Cordova Top (not applicable to Convertible)	75.32

Note: After December 1963, base prices increased $11.00 due to seat belts being issued as standard equipment.